THE PROPHETS STILL SPEAK

MESSIAH IN BOTH TESTAMENTS

by Fred John Meldau

The Friends of Israel Gospel Ministry, Inc.
P. O. Box 908, Bellmawr, NJ 08099

THE PROPHETS STILL SPEAK: MESSIAH IN BOTH TESTAMENTS
Fred John Meldau

Copyright © 1988 **The Christian Victory Publishing Co.**
2909 Umatilla Street, Denver, Colorado 80211

First Edition — 1956
Revised Edition — 1988
Revised Edition— 2003
Reprint — 2006
Reprint — 2012
Reprint — 2017

Permission to edit and reproduce granted to the Publisher:
The Friends of Israel Gospel Ministry, Inc.
P.O. Box 908 • Bellmawr, New Jersey 08099

Library of Congress Catalog Card Number 88-80834

ISBN-10 0-915540-42-8
ISBN-13 978-0-915540-42-6

Cover by Gariel Graphics, Woodbury, NJ

Visit our website at www.foi.org.

THE PROPHETS STILL SPEAK

MESSIAH IN BOTH TESTAMENTS

FOREWORD

Fred John Meldau's classic book, *Messiah in Both Testaments*, was used of God to touch thousands of lives over the years before going out of print.

Now, with special permission from the original publishers, we are pleased to offer it under a new title: *The Prophets Still Speak*.

We at The Friends of Israel are confident that your spiritual life and understanding will be enriched as you absorb this exceptional volume.

Elwood McQuaid
Former Executive Director
THE FRIENDS OF ISRAEL
GOSPEL MINISTRY, INC.

TABLE OF CONTENTS

Amazing Drama

To him give all the prophets witness (Acts 10:43).
In the volume of the book it is written of me (Ps. 40:7; Heb. 10:7).

"The most amazing drama that ever was presented to the mind of man—a drama written in prophecy in the Old Testament and in biography in the four Gospels of the New Testament—is the narrative of Jesus the Christ. One outstanding fact, among many, completely isolates Him. It is this: that one man only in the history of the world has had explicit details given beforehand of His birth, life, death and resurrection; that these details are in documents given to the public centuries before He appeared, and that no one challenges, or can challenge, that these documents were widely circulated long before His birth; and that anyone and everyone can compare for himself/herself the actual records of His life with those ancient documents, and find that they match one another perfectly. The challenge of this pure miracle is that it happened concerning one man in the whole history of the world" (D. M. Panton).

Scores of other Bible students have called attention to this same amazing fact. We quote from one more, Canon Dyson Hague. He says:

"Centuries before Christ was born His birth and career, His sufferings and glory, were all described in outline and detail in the Old Testament. Christ is the only person ever born into this world whose ancestry, birth time, forerunner, birthplace, birth manner, infancy, manhood, teaching character, career, preaching, reception, rejection, death, burial, resurrection and ascension were all prewritten in the most marvelous manner centuries before He was born.

"Who could draw a picture of a man not yet born? Surely God, and God alone. Nobody knew 500 years ago that Shakespeare was going to be born; or 250 years ago that Napoleon was to be born. Yet here in the Bible we have the most striking and unmistakable likeness of a man portrayed, not by one, but by twenty or twenty-five artists, none of whom had ever seen the man they were painting."

To focus attention on the unparalleled wonder of this literary miracle, think for a moment. Who could have prewritten the life of George Washington, Abraham Lincoln or any other character 500 years before he was born? Nowhere in any of the literature of the world, secular or religious, can one find a duplicate to the astounding miracle of the prewritten life of Christ. "The inspiration of that portrait came from the heavenly gallery, and not from the studio of an earthly artist" (A. T. Pierson). So amazing is this miracle of the prewritten life of Christ and its prefect fulfillment in the Lord Jesus that, "Nothing but divine prescience could have foreseen it, and nothing but divine power could accomplish it." As the full evidence is presented, it becomes obvious that, "the prophecy came not at any time by the will of man, but holy men of God spoke as they were moved by the Holy Spirit" (2 Pet. 1:21).

Four Great Truths Demonstrated by This Fact

With no variations or aberrations between the Old Testament predictions of the coming Messiah and the New Testament fulfillment in Jesus of Nazareth, one instinctively leaps to the conclusion that the hand that drew the image in prophecy molded the portrait in history; and the inevitable result of this miracle is fourfold.

First, it proves that the Bible is the inspired Word of God, for unaided man is neither capable of writing nor of fulfilling such a literary wonder.

Second, it proves that the God of the Bible, the only One who knows the end from the beginning, and who alone has the power to fulfill all His Word, is the true and living God.

Third, it proves that the God of the Bible is both all-knowing (able to foretell the future entwined around numberless men who are free moral agents) and all-powerful (able to bring to pass a perfect fulfillment of His Word in the midst of widespread unbelief, ignorance and rebellion on the part of men).

Fourth, it proves that Jesus, who so perfectly and completely fulfilled all the Old Testament predictions, is indeed the Messiah, the Savior of the world, the Son of the living God.

Christ is, therefore, seen to be the center of all history as well as the central reality of the Bible. "The Christ of the New Testament is the fruit of the tree of prophecy, and Christianity is the realization of a plan, the first outlines of which were sketched more than 1,500 years before" (David Baron, *Rays of Messiah's Glory*, p. 14).

Fulfilled Prophecy is Unique to the Bible

The fact of fulfilled prophecy is found in the Bible alone; hence, it presents proof of divine inspiration that is positive, conclusive and overwhelming. Here is the argument in brief.

No man, unaided by divine inspiration, foreknows the future, for it is an impenetrable wall to all mankind. Only an all-powerful and an all-knowing God can infallibly predict the future. If, then, one can find true prophecy (as one does in the Bible), with proven fulfillment, sufficient time intervening between the prediction and the fulfillment, and explicit details in the prediction to assure that the prophecies are not clever guesses, then the case is perfect. There were 400 years between the last of the messianic predictions of the Old Testament and their fulfillment in the Christ of the Gospels. Many prophecies are, of course, much older than 400 B.C. During the period of 1,100 years from the time of Moses (1500 B.C.) to that of Malachi (400 B.C.), a succession of prophets arose, messianic prediction took form, and all of them testified of the Messiah who was to come.

The perfect proof of the long period of time that elapsed between the last book of the Old Testament and the first book of the New Testament is the presence in the world of the *Septuagint*, a translation of the Old Testament into Greek. This translation was begun during the reign of Ptolemy Philadelphus in about 280 B.C. and was completed not long thereafter. With a translation of the entire Old Testament, as we now know it, made more than 200 years before Christ, it is obvious that the books of the Old Testament, from which the translation was made, are still older.

Moreover, there were no prophets in the 400-year intertestament period. In 1 Maccabees 9:27 we are told of the "great affliction in Israel, such as there was not since the day that a prophet was not seen among them." Intense regret over the lack of a prophet merged into an intense longing for the coming again of prophets, so that even in their public actions men were careful to claim validity for their legislation only until a faithful prophet should again arise (see 1 Macc. 4:46; 14:41).

So specific and so voluminous are these Old Testament predictions, and so complete is their fulfillment in the New Testament, that Dr. A. T. Pierson says: "There would be no honest infidel in the world were messianic prophecy studied . . . nor would there be any doubting disciples if this fact of prediction and fulfillment were fully understood. And, the sad fact is, we have yet to meet the first honest skeptic or critic who has carefully studied the prophecies which center in Christ" (*Many Infallible Proofs*). Here indeed is God's rock of ages, faith's unshakable standing place.

Prophecy is God's Own Method of Proving His Truth

The teachings of the Bible are so peculiar and different from all other religions and so important—telling us that man's eternal destiny, for weal or woe, depends on his acceptance of the Christ of the Bible—that it is appropriate that we know whether the Bible is or is not a heavenly decree, the absolute and final Word of God, and whether its message is fully authorized by the Almighty. If God has given a revelation of His will in the Bible, there can be no doubt that in some unmistakable way He will show men that the Bible is indeed His revealed will; and the way He has chosen to show men that the Bible is His Word is through the giving and subsequent fulfillment of specific, detailed prophecies. This specific fulfillment is the divine seal, letting all men know that He has spoken. This seal can never be counterfeited, for His foreknowledge of the actions of free and intelligent agents—men—is one of the most "incomprehensible attributes of deity and is exclusively a divine perfection" (Alexander Keith, *Evidences of Prophecy*, p. 8).

In challenging the false gods of Isaiah's time, the true God said: "Produce your cause . . . bring forth your strong reasons . . . show us what shall happen . . . declare us things to come. Show the things that are to come hereafter, that we may know that ye are gods" (Isa. 41:21–23).

There are false faiths, such as Mohammedianism and Buddhism, which have tried to prop up their claims on pretended miracles, but neither of these, nor any other religious scripture in the history of the world, apart from the Bible, has ever ventured to frame prophecies.

It is the peculiar glory of the Almighty, the all-knowing God, who is "the LORD, the Creator" (Isa. 40:28) to declare "new things . . . before they spring forth" (Isa. 42:9) and that glory He will not share with another (Isa. 42:8). The true God alone foreknows and foretells the future, and He has chosen to confine His foretelling to the pages of Scripture.

Many have made an effort to foretell the future—not one, apart from the Bible, has ever succeeded. "The extreme difficulty of framing a prophecy which shall prove accurate may be seen in that familiar but crude rhyme known as 'Mother Shipton's Prophecy.' Some years ago it appeared as a pretended relic of a remote day and claimed to have predicted the invention of the steam locomotive, the rise of D'Israeli in English politics, etc., etc. . . . For years I tried to unearth and expose what seemed to me a huge impostor, and I succeeded . . . I traced the whole thing to one Charles Hindley (of England) who acknowledged himself the author of this prophetic hoax, which was written in 1862 instead of 1448, and palmed off on a credulous public. It is one of the startling proofs of human perversity that the very people who will try to cast suspicion on prophecies two thousand years old will, without straining, swallow a forgery that was first published *after* the events it predicted, and will not even look into its claim to antiquity" (Dr. A. T. Pierson, *Many Infallible Proofs*, pp. 44–45).

Although there are many other subjects of divine prophecy in the Bible (i.e., the Jews, the Gentile nations which surrounded Israel, ancient cities, the Church, the last days, etc.), the divine perfections of foreknowledge and fulfillment can be seen better in the realm of prophecies concerning Christ than in any other sphere.

Here is a clear statement that God alone, in the Bible alone, gives true prophecies:

I am God, and there is none else; I am God, and there is none like me, declaring the end from the beginning, and from ancient times the things that are not yet done, saying, My counsel shall stand, and I will do all my pleasure (Isa. 46:9–10).

This declaration by God that He alone can give and fulfill prophecy, and that prophecy is to be found only in the Bible, is found in many other places in the Bible (see Dt. 18:21–22; Isa. 41:21–23; Jer. 28:9; Jn. 13:19; 2 Tim. 3:16; 2 Pet. 1:19–21; etc.).

Sensing the tremendous force of this fact, Justin Martyr said, "To declare a thing shall come to pass long before it is in being, and to bring it to pass, this or nothing is the work of God."

Chance Fulfillment of Prophecy is Ruled Out

Atheists and other unbelievers, seeking a way to circumvent the fact of fulfilled prophecy and its connotations, have argued that the fulfillments were *accidental, chance* or *coincidental.* But when such complete details are given, the *chance* fulfillment of prophecy is ruled out. One writer says:

It is conceivable that a prediction, uttered at a venture and expressing what in a general way may happen to result, may seem like a genuine prophecy. But only let the prophecy give several *details* of time, place and accompanying incidents, and it is evident that the possibility of a chance fulfillment, by a 'fortuitous concurrence of events,' will become extremely desperate—yea, altogether impossible. Hence, the prophecies of heathen antiquity always took good care to confine their predictions to one or two particulars and to express them in the most general and ambiguous terms. Therefore, in the whole range of history, except the prophecies of Scripture, *there is not a single instance of a prediction, expressed in unequivocal language and descending to any minuteness, which bears the slightest claim to fulfillment.* 'Suppose,' says Dr. Olinthus Gregory, 'that there were only 50 prophecies in the Old Testament (instead of 333) concerning the first advent of Christ, giving details of the coming Messiah and all meet in the person of Jesus . . . the probability of chance fulfillment as calculated by mathematicians according to the theory of probabilities is less than one in 1,125,000,000,000,000. Now add only two more elements to these 50 prophecies and fix the *time* and *place* at which they must happen, and the *immense improbability that they will take place by chance exceeds all the power of numbers to express* (or the mind of man to grasp). This is enough, one would think, to silence forever all pleas for *chance* as furnishing an unbeliever the least opportunity of escape from the evidence of prophecy' (Gregory's Letters) [Alexander Keith, *Evidences of Prophecy,* p. 8].

Let it be further observed that many of the prophecies about the Messiah are of such a nature that only God *could* fulfill them (i.e., His virgin birth, His sinless and holy character, His resurrection and His ascension). Only God could cause Jesus "to be born of a virgin or be raised from the dead" (David Baron).

The Coming Messiah

In the Old Testament there is a definite, clear and continuous teaching that the Messiah will come. Dozens of times we read such promises as, "behold, thy King cometh unto thee" (Zech. 9:9); "the Lord GOD will come" (Isa. 40:10); "the Lord, whom ye seek, shall suddenly come to his temple" (Mal. 3:1); "The LORD thy God will raise up unto thee a Prophet from the midst of thee" (Dt. 18:15–19); the "Prophet" will be the Lord's "fellow" (equal) [Zech. 13:7]. Daniel predicted the coming of "Messiah, the Prince" at a set time (Dan. 9:25–26), and Isaiah foretold the "rod out of the stem of Jesse" (Isa. 11:1) on whom the Lord would lay "the iniquity of us all" (Isa. 53:6). Prophets and seers of old often spoke of the time when "the desire of all nations" would come (Hag. 2:7; see also Gen. 3:15; 49:10; Num. 24:17; Ps. 2:5–6; 118:26; Isa. 35:4; 62:11; Jer. 23:5–6).

The coming of Christ, promised in the Old Testament and fulfilled in the New—His birth, character, work, teachings, sufferings, death and resurrection—are the grand, central themes of the Bible. Christ is the bond that ties the two Testaments together. The Old Testament is in the New revealed; the New Testament is in the Old concealed.

A. T. Pierson says:

The most ordinary reader may examine the old curious predictions of the Messiah's person and work found in the Old Testament, follow the gradual progress of these revelations from Genesis to Malachi, and trace the prophecies as they descend into details more and more specific and minute, until at last the full figure of the coming One stands out. Then, with this image clearly fixed in his mind's eye, he may turn to the New Testament and beginning with Matthew, see how the *historic* personage, Jesus of Nazareth, corresponds and coincides in every particular with the *prophetic* personage depicted by the prophets. . . . There is not a difference or a divergence, yet there could have been no collusion or contact between the prophets of the Old Testament and the narrators of the New Testament. Observe, the reader has not gone out of the Bible itself. He has simply compared two portraits, one in the Old Testament of a mysterious coming One and another in the New of One who has actually come, and his irresistible conclusion is that these two blend in absolute unity.

A Brief Summary of the Prophecies

Let us briefly trace a few of the outstanding points in the comparison of Old Testament prediction and New Testament fulfillment. The work of redemption was to be accomplished by one person, the central figure in both Testaments, the promised Messiah. As the *seed of the woman*, He was to bruise Satan's head (Gen. 3:15; cp. Gal. 4:4). As the *seed of Abraham* (Gen. 22:18; cp. Gal. 3:16). As the *seed of David* (Ps. 132:11; Jer. 23:5; cp. Acts 13:23), He was to come from the tribe of Judah (Gen. 49:10; cp. Heb. 7:14).

The Messiah was to come at a specific time (Gen. 49:10; Dan. 9:24–25; cp. Lk. 2:1–2) and be born of a virgin (Isa. 7:14; cp. Mt. 1:18–23) in Bethlehem of Judea (Mic. 5:2; cp. Mt. 2:1; Lk. 2:4–5). Great persons were to visit and adore Him (Ps. 72:10; cp. Mt. 2:1–11). Through the rage of a jealous king, innocent children were to be slaughtered (Jer. 31:15; cp. Mt. 2:16–18).

He was to be preceded by a forerunner, John the Baptist, before entering His public ministry (Isa. 40:3; Mal. 3:1; cp. Mt. 3:1–3; Lk. 1:17). He was to be a prophet like Moses (Dt. 18:18; cp. Acts 3:20–22) and have a special anointing of the Holy Spirit (Ps. 45:7; Isa. 11:2; 61:1–2; cp. Mt. 3:16; Lk. 4:15–21, 43). He was to be a priest after the order of Melchizedek (Ps. 110:4; cp. Heb. 5:5–6). As the servant of the Lord, He was to be a faithful and patient Redeemer, for the Gentiles as well as the Jews (Isa. 42:1–4; cp. Mt. 12:18–21).

The Messiah's ministry was to begin in Galilee (Isa. 9:1–2; cp. Mt. 4:12–17, 23). Later He was to enter Jerusalem (Zech. 9:9; cp. Mt. 21:1–5) to bring salvation. He was also to enter the Temple (Hag. 2:7–9; Mal. 3:1; cp. Mt. 21:12).

His zeal for the Lord was to be remarkable (Ps. 69:9; cp. Jn. 2:17). His manner of teaching was to be by parables (Ps. 78:2; cp. Mt. 13:34–35), and His ministry was to be characterized by miracles (Isa. 35:5–6; cp. Mt. 11:4–6; Jn. 11:47). He was to be rejected by His brethren (Ps. 69:8; Isa. 53:3; cp. Jn. 1:11; 7:5) and be a "stone of stumbling" to the Jews and a "rock of offense" (Isa. 8:14; cp. Rom. 9:32–33; 1 Pet. 2:8).

The Messiah was to be hated without a cause (Ps. 69:4; Isa. 49:7; cp. Jn. 7:48; 15:25), rejected by the rulers (Ps. 118:22; cp. Mt. 21:42), betrayed by a friend (Ps. 41:9; 55:12–13; cp. Jn. 13:18, 21), forsaken by His disciples (Zech. 13:7; cp. Mt. 26:31, 56), sold for 30 pieces of silver (Zech. 11:12; cp. Mt. 26:15) and His price given for the potter's field (Zech. 11:13; cp. Mt. 27:3, 7). He was to be smitten on the cheek (Mic. 5:1; cp. Mt. 27:30), spat upon (Isa. 50:6; cp. Mt. 27:30), mocked (Ps. 22:7–8; cp. Mt. 27:31, 39–44) and beaten (Isa. 50:6 ff.; cp Mt. 26:67; 27:26, 30).

It is most impressive to read in parallel statements the prediction in comparison with the fulfillment. For example, compare the following Old Testament and New Testament passages.

PROPHECY:
I gave my back to the smiters, and my cheeks to them that plucked off the hair; I hid not my face from shame and spitting (Isa. 50:6).

FULFILLMENT:
Then they spat in his face, and buffeted him; and others smote him with the palms of their hands (Mt. 26:67).

The Messiah's death by crucifixion is given in detail in Psalm 22, and the meaning of His death as a substitutionary atonement is given in Isaiah 53. His hands and feet were to be pierced (Ps. 22:16; Zech. 12:10; cp. Jn. 19:18, 37; 20:25); yet not one of His bones was to be broken (Ex. 12:46; Ps. 34:20; cp. Jn. 19:33–36). He was to suffer thirst (Ps. 22:15; cp. Jn. 19:28) and be given vinegar to drink (Ps. 69:21; cp. Mt. 27:34); and He was to be numbered with transgressors (Isa. 53:12; cp. Mt. 27:38).

The Messiah's body was to be buried with the rich in His death (Isa. 53:9; cp. Mt. 27:57–60) but was not to see corruption (Ps. 16:10; Acts 2:31).

He was to be raised from the dead (Ps. 2:7; 16:10; cp. Act. 13:33) and ascend to the right hand of God (Ps. 68:18; cp. Lk. 24:51; Acts 1:9; also Ps. 110:1; cp. Heb. 1:3).

This brief sketch of Old Testament messianic prophecies with their New Testament fulfillments is, of course, far from complete; it is merely suggestive, although many of the main points have been covered. There are actually 333 predictions concerning the coming Messiah in the Old Testament!

It is valuable to gather together, as in a great museum, at least some of the prophetic masterpieces scattered throughout the realm of the entire 39 books of the Old Testament, so that one can get a view of them in one group without having to travel laboriously throughout hundreds of pages of Scripture.

The Messiah Who Has Come

Christ's Testimony to the Fact that He Fulfilled Old Testament Prophecy

The golden milestone in the ancient city of Rome was the point in the old world at which the many roads, running from all directions in the Roman Empire, met and converged. In like manner, all lines of Old Testament messianic prophecy meet in Jesus, the Christ of the New Testament.

Not only was the life of Christ prewritten in the Old Testament, but Jesus knew it and fully witnessed to that fact in the New Testament. This is a miracle in itself and finds no parallel in the literature of the world. No other character of history—Caesar, Gladstone, Shakespeare or any other—ever dreamed of saying of the Bible or any other book, as our Lord did, "Search the scriptures; for they . . . testify of me" (Jn. 5:39). Nor has any false Christ ever appealed to fulfilled prophecy to vindicate his claims.

In *Rays of Messiah's Glory* (p. 46), David Baron calls attention to the fact that "More than forty false Messiahs have appeared in the history of the Jewish nation," and *not one of them* ever appealed to fulfilled prophecy to establish his claims. Rather, they bolstered their fake claims by "promises of revenge and by flatteries which gratified national vanity. And now, except to a few students of history, the remembrance of their names has perished from the earth, while Jesus of Nazareth, the true Messiah, who fulfilled all the prophecies, is worshiped by hundreds of millions."

Thus, Christianity is not a new religion unconnected to the Old Testament. It is based solidly on being the *fulfillment* of the Old Testament promises. "Christianity, with its central figure human and divine, Prophet, Priest and King, is nothing less than the translation of prophecy from the region of ardent belief to actual fact . . . and we see the living and organic connection between the two dispensations and recognize it is the same God who spake in both—in the first to prepare, in the second to accomplish. . . .'Known unto God are all his works from the beginning of the age' (Acts 15:18)" [E. A. Edghill, *The Value of Prophecy*, pp. 389–390].

Jesus calmly said, "Abraham . . . saw . . . my day" (Jn. 8:56) and "Moses . . . wrote of me" (Jn. 5:46). To show the connection between Old Testament prediction and New Testament fulfillment, He said in His

Sermon on the Mount, "Think not that I am come to destroy the law, or the prophets . . . but to fulfill" (Mt. 5:17).

The life of Christ was unique; all was according to the divine pattern as given in the Old Testament. He was the One sent by the Father to fulfill all His will, to accomplish His work as Redeemer, and to fulfill all the prophecies concerning Him (Jn. 3:16–17; Heb. 10:9; 1 Jn. 4:14).

In the beginning of His ministry, after reading to the people in the synagogue in Nazareth the important Messianic prophecy in Isaiah 61:1–2, when all eyes were fastened on Him, He said, "This day is this scripture fulfilled in your ears" (Lk. 4:16–21). When talking to Jesus at the well, the woman of Samaria said, "I know that Messiah cometh, who is called Christ; [all devout readers of the Old Testament knew that], when he is come, he will tell us all things. Jesus saith unto her, I that speak unto thee am he" (Jn. 4:25–26). When Peter confessed his faith in Jesus as the Messiah—"Thou art the Christ, the Son of the living God" (Mt. 16:16)—the Lord Jesus acknowledged the truth of what he had said by answering, "Blessed art thou, Simon Bar-jona; for flesh and blood hath not revealed it unto thee, but my Father, who is in heaven" (Mt. 16:17).

Jesus quoted from Psalm 110 to identify Himself as the "Son of David" (a messianic title) and also to prove that David called Him "Lord" (Ps. 110:1; cp. Mt. 22:41–46). By taking the title "Son of man," He identified Himself with that messianic title used in Daniel (Dan. 7:13; cp. Mk. 14:62). By taking the title "Son of God," He identified Himself with that messianic title used in Psalm 2.

He connected the blessings of salvation given to all who trust in Him with the promises of the Old Testament, "He that believeth on me, as the scripture hath said, out of his heart shall flow rivers of living water" (Jn. 7:38). Here the Lord was speaking of the fulfillment, *through Himself*, of the type in the Feast of Tabernacles (see context, Jn. 7:37; Lev. 23:34–36; Isa. 12:3).

Almost everything Christ said or did had some connection with Old Testament prophecy. His miracles were in fulfillment of Old Testament predictions (Isa. 35:5–6); His ministry corresponded with what Isaiah had predicted concerning Him (Isa. 42:1–4; 61:1–3; cp. Mt. 12:17–21). His sufferings and death at Jerusalem were all in accordance with what had been foretold (Ps. 22; Isa. 53). When praising John the Baptist, Jesus called attention to the fact that John was His forerunner—"For this is he [John the Baptist] of whom it is written, Behold, I send my messenger

before thy face, who shall prepare thy way before thee" (Mt. 11:10)—
which had been predicted in Isaiah 40:3 and Malachi 3:1. The Lord was
saying that not only did *John* come in fulfillment of prophecy, but that
He was the One for whom John came to be a forerunner!

As He drew near to the cross, Jesus said to His disciples, "Behold, we
go up to Jerusalem, and all things that are written by the prophets concerning the Son of man shall be accomplished" (Lk. 18:31). On the eve of
His crucifixion He said, "this that is written must yet be accomplished
in me, And he was reckoned among the transgressors; for the things
concerning me have a fulfillment" (Lk. 22:37). Note the word "must."

During the crucial hours of His trial, Jesus said to Peter (who was
willing to defend his Master with his sword), "Thinkest thou that I cannot now pray to my Father, and he shall presently give me more than
twelve legions of angels? But how, then, shall the scriptures be fulfilled,
that thus it must be?" (Mt. 26:53–54). Then, chiding the multitudes, He
said, "Are ye come out as against a thief with swords and clubs to take
me? I sat daily with you teaching in the temple, and ye laid no hold on
me. But all this was done, that the scriptures of the prophets might be
fulfilled" (Mt. 26:55–56). At His trial, when the high priest put Him
under oath and asked, "Art thou the Christ, the Son of the Blessed?"
Jesus answered, "I am" (Mk. 14:61–62).

Suffering on the cross, the Lord Jesus identified Himself as the One
whose hands and feet were to be pierced (Ps. 22:16) and quoted Psalm
22:1, "My God, my God, why hast thou forsaken me?" Three of His
seven sayings on the cross were the very words of Scripture.

After His resurrection, while talking to His two disciples on the
Emmaus road, "beginning at Moses and all the prophets, he expounded
unto them, in all the scriptures, the things concerning himself" (Lk.
24:27). And later, when meeting with the assembled disciples, He said,
"These are the words which I spoke unto you, while I was yet with you,
that all things must be fulfilled, which were written in the law of Moses,
and in the prophets, and in the psalms, concerning me" (Lk. 24:44).

On various occasions, the Lord spoke of the necessity—"must"—of
Old Testament prophecy being fulfilled in Him. This was necessary
because the Word of God cannot fail, the God of the Word cannot lie,
and the Son of God who fulfilled the Word cannot fail. "The scripture
cannot be broken" (Jn. 10:35).

After His resurrection, the Lord gave His disciples the key that
unlocks messianic prophecy in the Old Testament: "And [He] said unto

them, Thus it is written, and thus it behooved Christ to suffer, and to rise from the dead the third day; And that repentance and remission of sins should be preached in his name among all nations" (Lk. 24:46–47). This great statement is a summary of His teachings during the 40 days He ministered to His disciples between His resurrection and ascension. The Jewish people of His day, and to this day, looked for a triumphant, reigning Messiah and failed to see from their own Scriptures that Christ must *suffer* for the sins of the world before entering His glory.

Peter bore the same testimony of the witness of the Holy Spirit through the prophets of the Old Testament when He testified beforehand of "the sufferings of Christ, and the glory that should follow" (1 Pet. 1:11).

The Apostles and Writers of the New Testament Also Bear Witness that Jesus the Christ Fulfilled Old Testament Prophecies

Many modern Christians have lost—or never had—an enlightened understanding of the genius of Christianity: that the New Testament is the fulfillment of the predictions and promises of the Old; that Jesus, the Christ, is the link binding the two Testaments together. The early New Testament church writers and preachers saw this clearly and constantly pointed out the New Testament fulfillment of Old Testament prophecy.

When Matthew narrated the virgin birth of Christ in Matthew 1:18–25, he said it was the fulfillment of the Old Testament prediction of Messiah's virgin birth: "Now all this was done, that it might be fulfilled which was spoken by the Lord through the prophet, saying, Behold, the virgin shall be with child, and shall bring forth a son, and they shall call his name Immanuel, which, being interpreted, is God with us" (Mt. 1:22–23; cp. Isa. 7:14).

When King Herod, in a jealous rage, slaughtered the innocent children in his vain effort to kill the Christ child, Matthew called attention to the fact that even this gruesome murder was predicted by God and then fulfilled (Mt. 2:16–18; cp. Jer. 31:15).

In dozens of places in the Gospels, the evangelists imply or state that Jesus fulfilled Old Testament prophecy. Peter expressed the convictions of the other disciples when he made his great confession, "Thou art the Christ, the Son of the living God" (Mt. 16:16; cp. Mt. 8:17; 12:17–18; etc.).

The main theme of the Gospel of John, as well as all four Gospels, is to prove that Jesus was the predicted Messiah, the Son of God, the One who was to come. "But these are written, that ye might believe that Jesus is the Christ, the Son of God; and that believing ye might have life through his name" (Jn. 20:31).

The purpose of John's Gospel is to show that Jesus has all the qualifications, the character and the works of the Messiah—Jesus fulfills all that was written of the Messiah—hence, He is the Messiah.

All of the apostles "laid great stress upon this argument from prophecy: it was not only the main, but almost the sole, argument employed in the New Testament . . . [They felt] it necessary to show the marvelous correspondence between the well-known *facts* [of the life, death and resurrection of Christ] with Old Testament prophecy, in order to carry conviction to every fair mind; and so this was the common method of preaching the gospel, the solid but simple base of argument upon which rested all appeal" (A. T. Pierson, *Many Infallible Proofs*, p. 187).

The backbone of Peter's sermon on the day of Pentecost was an argument from the Old Testament to prove to the Jews that Jesus of Nazareth, whom they had crucified but whom God had raised from the dead, *was the Messiah about whom David had written,* and that this God had raised Him up and made Him "both Lord and Christ" (Acts 2:22–36).

In Peter's second sermon recorded in the Book of Acts and delivered at the gate of the Temple, he proved his argument by saying: "And now, brethren, I know that through ignorance ye did it [rejected and killed Jesus, the Messiah], as did also your rulers. But those things, which God had shown by the mouth of all his prophets, that Christ should suffer, he hath so fulfilled. Repent, therefore, and be converted, that your sins may be blotted out" (Acts 3:17–19).

Even in his sermon to the assembled Gentiles in the house of Cornelius, Peter said: "To him [Jesus] give all the prophets witness, that through his name whosoever believeth in him shall receive remission of sin" (Acts 10:43).

In Paul's sermon in the synagogue at Antioch he said: "And when they had fulfilled all that was written of him, they took him down from the tree, and laid him in a sepulcher. But God raised him from the dead" (Acts 13:29–30).

Paul's method of preaching the gospel to the Jews is given in Acts 17:2–3: "And Paul, as his manner was, went in unto them, and three sabbath days reasoned with them out of the scriptures [Old Testament],

Opening and alleging that Christ [Messiah] must needs have suffered, and risen again from the dead; and that this Jesus, whom I preach unto you, is Christ" (Act. 17:2–3).

When Paul defined the gospel by which people are saved, he connected the New Testament facts of the death and resurrection of Christ with Old Testament prediction and teaching: "Moreover, brethren, I declare unto you the gospel . . . By which also ye are saved . . . that Christ died for our sins according to the scriptures [Old Testament]; And that he was buried, and that he rose again the third day according to the scriptures" (1 Cor. 15:1–4).

Thus, the writers and preachers of the New Testament constantly pointed out that Jesus lived, suffered, died and rose again in fulfillment of Old Testament prophecy. Commenting on this fact, Dr. A. T. Pierson said, "No miracle which He wrought so unmistakably set on Jesus the seal of God as the convergence of the thousand lines of prophecy in Him, as in one burning focal point of dazzling glory. Every sacrifice presented, from the hour of Abel's altar fire down to the last Passover lamb of the passion week, pointed as with flaming finger to Calvary's cross. Nay, all the centuries moved as in solemn procession to lay their tributes upon Golgotha."

Looked at in more detail and divided into different categories, one can demonstrate that all messianic predictions of the Old Testament converge in Jesus of Nazareth as a "focal point of dazzling glory."

Prophecies Establishing
the Credentials of the Messiah

Credentials are testimonials, written proofs, proving the bearer to right of office or position. Our gracious Redeemer, when He came to the earth, condescended to present His *credentials* from the heavenly court. These credentials prove that Jesus is the Christ. In the first chapter of Matthew, he presents a succinct summary of His credentials, "The book of the genealogy of Jesus Christ, the son of David, the son of Abraham" (Mt. 1:1).

By giving a sufficient number of definite *specifications* in the Old Testament concerning the coming Messiah, God enabled us to pick out one man from all history, from all nations, from all peoples, and be absolutely sure that one man is the Messiah! These details of His credentials, these specifications, these elements of His *address*, were given that all might know who the true Messiah is. As these prophecies are listed and explained, it soon becomes obvious that no other person in the history of the world could fulfill them all—or even a very small percentage of them—other than Jesus.

Very early on in the biblical narrative, God eliminated *half* of the human race as the immediate parent of the Messiah; and at the same time He made it clear that the Messiah would come as a man and not

as an angel when He gave the promise that the coming Deliverer would
be the *seed of the woman*:

> *And I will put enmity between thee and the woman, and between thy*
> *seed and her seed; he shall bruise thy head, and thou shalt bruise his heel*
> (Gen. 3:15).

This, the first of the direct messianic promises in the Bible, is "the
Bible in embryo, the sum of all history and prophecy in a germ" (H.
Grattan Guinness, *The Approaching End of the Age*). Here is foretold not
only the virgin birth of Christ but also His vicarious sufferings—"thou
shalt bruise his heel"—and His complete, eventual victory over Satan
and his works—"he [the Messiah] shall bruise thy head."

There is further remarkable evidence in Genesis 4:1 that this promise in
Genesis 3:15 was well-understood by Adam and Eve, for at the birth of
her first son, Eve ecstatically exclaimed, "I have obtained the man, even
the Lord!" (Heb. of Gen. 4:1). When her firstborn son arrived, Eve thought
the promised Deliverer had come. But she was mistaken as to the time,
place and many other yet-to-be-revealed specifications. Many centuries
must pass before the Messiah could come. "But, when the fullness of the
time was come, God sent forth his Son, made of a woman, made under
the law, To redeem them that were under the law" (Gal. 4:4–5).

Then God eliminated two-thirds of the nations by indicating that the
Messiah must come through Noah's son *Shem*, not Ham or Japheth.

In the very beginning of the history of the nations, God, through His
prophet Noah, identified Himself with Shem in a special way:

> *Blessed be the* LORD *God of Shem . . . God shall enlarge Japheth, and he*
> *shall dwell in the tents of Shem* (Gen. 9:26–27).

In the Hebrew of Genesis 9:27, there is no word corresponding to
"he" as found in the King James Version; therefore, the verse correctly
reads, "God will enlarge Japheth, and will dwell in the tents of Shem."
The *Chaldee of Onkelos* paraphrase of the verse reads, "and will make his
glory to dwell in the tabernacles of Shem." The final fulfillment of the
prediction in Genesis 9:27 came when the eternal Word, who was with
God and was God (Jn. 1:1), "was made flesh, and dwelt among us (and
we beheld his glory, the glory as of the only begotten of the Father), full
of grace and truth" (Jn. 1:14). He came to His people Israel, who are
descendants of Shem, through Abraham (see Gen. 11:10–27).

Later still, another choice was made by God. All of the hundreds of
nations of the world were eliminated except one, the new nation begun
by God himself when He called Abraham. God divided the nations into

two groups, Jewish and Gentile, and separated one small nation, the Jewish nation, that through it the Messiah might come.

Now the LORD had said unto Abram, Get thee out of thy country, and from thy kindred, and from thy father's house, unto a land that I will show thee; And I will make of thee a great nation, and I will bless thee, and make thy name great; and thou shalt be a blessing. And I will bless them that bless thee, and curse him that curseth thee: and in thee shall all families of the earth be blessed . . . Unto thy seed will I give this land (Gen. 12:1–3, 7; cp. Gen. 17:1–8).

And the angel of the LORD called unto Abraham out of heaven the second time, And said, By myself have I sworn, saith the LORD . . . That in blessing I will bless thee . . . And in thy seed shall all the nations of the earth be blessed (Gen. 22:16–18).

Here is a phenomenon of the first magnitude, a record that goes back 1,500 years before Christ *in which the writer hazards multiple predictions* that God would bless Abraham, make him a blessing, give him the land of Canaan and bless the world through him and his "seed." A great nation was created and given a land of their own for one purpose—so that the Messiah might come to and through them to bless the world! The prediction has been in the Book of Genesis, unchanged, for thousands of years.

Its fulfillment is an age-long miracle and is as definite and complete as the original prophecy. Not only did God make of Abraham a great nation, giving Canaan to the Jewish under the conquest of Joshua, but in due time the Messiah came to them, and the world has been immeasurably blessed through Abraham's seed, which is Christ. Concerning this subject, we read in the Book of Galatians:

And the scripture, foreseeing that God would justify the Gentiles through faith, preached before the gospel unto Abraham, saying, In thee shall all nations be blessed . . . Now to Abraham and his seed were the promises made. He saith not, And to seeds, as of many; but as of one, And to thy seed, which is Christ (Gal. 3:8, 16).

And so, the messianic story slowly unfolded in the Old Testament. The Messiah must be the *seed of the woman,* come through the *line of Shem,* and be the *seed of Abraham.* That narrowed the search for the Messiah. Men knew to look for Him in the Jewish race, as a descendant of Abraham.

Abraham, however, had several sons, including Ishmael, his firstborn, and Isaac. Another choice was therefore made, and the line narrowed still more. The Messiah would come through Isaac (Gen. 17:19; 21:12; cp. Heb. 11:18; Rom. 9:7, "in Isaac shall thy seed be called") and not through Ishmael, the progenitor of the modern Arabs.

And the LORD appeared unto him [Isaac], and said, Go not down into Egypt; dwell in the land which I shall tell thee of. Sojourn in this land, and I will be with thee, and will bless thee; for unto thee, and unto thy seed, I will give all these countries [the promised land], and I will perform the oath which I swore unto Abraham thy father; And I will make thy seed to multiply as the stars of heaven, and will give unto thy seed all these countries; and in thy seed shall all the nations of the earth be blessed (Gen. 26:2–4).

That the Messiah and the promised blessing must come through Isaac and the Jewish race, not the Arabs, is further emphasized in Deuteronomy 18:15–18, where it is specifically prophesied that the Messiah, the great Prophet yet to come, would be raised up "from the midst of thee [Israel], of thy brethren." This fact is also clearly set forth in the New Testament: "Who are Israelites . . . Whose are the fathers, and of whom, as concerning the flesh, Christ came, who is over all, God blessed forever" (Rom. 9:4–5).

Since Isaac had two sons, the messianic line was again narrowed through the clear prediction that that the Messiah would come through Jacob, not Esau; that is, the Messiah could not be an Edomite (the descendants of Esau).

And, behold, the LORD . . . said, I am the LORD God of Abraham, thy father, and the God of Isaac: the land whereon thou liest, to thee will I give it, and to thy seed . . . and in thee and in thy seed shall all the families of the earth be blessed (Gen. 28:13–14).

I shall see him, but not now: I shall behold him, but not near: there shall come a Star out of Jacob, and a Scepter shall rise out of Israel . . . Out of Jacob shall he come who shall have dominion (Num. 24:17, 19).

But Jacob had twelve sons, so another choice had to be made by the Almighty. One of the twelve, *Judah*, was selected. The Messiah would come, not from the other eleven tribes of Israel:

The scepter shall not depart from Judah, nor a lawgiver from between his feet, until Shiloh come; and unto him shall the gathering of the people be (Gen. 49:10).

For Judah prevailed above his brethren, and of him came the prince (1 Chr. 5:2; note that the word "prince" in the original is *Nagid*, the same word applied to the Messiah in Dan. 9:25).

Moreover, he refused the tabernacle of Joseph, and chose not the tribe of Ephraim; But chose the tribe of Judah (Ps. 78:67–68).

In the New Testament we read that Jesus "sprang out of Judah (Heb. 7:14; cp. Rev. 5:5).

Next, of the thousands of families in the tribe of Judah, the Lord made another choice: The Messiah must come from one family line, the *family of Jesse.*

And there shall come forth a rod out of the stem of Jesse, and a Branch shall grow out of his roots; And the Spirit of the LORD shall rest upon him (Isa. 11:1–2).

The word "rod" appears in only one other Old Testament passage (Prov. 14:3) and means *a twig, a shoot such as starts up from the roots of a cut-down tree stump.* Isaiah 11:1–2 is a clear statement that God will take a man with no standing—a mere *stump* of a tree cut down—and graft new life into it. Jesse was not the head of a royal family until God made him the father of a king and put him into the messianic line!

Since Jesse had eight sons, another divine choice was made. The Messiah was to be a descendant of *David,* Jesse's youngest son.

I will set up thy seed after thee, which shall proceed out of thine own body, and I will establish his kingdom. He shall build an house for my name, and I will establish the throne of his kingdom forever (2 Sam. 7:12–13; cp. 1 Chr. 17:11, 14; Ps. 89:35–37; Jer. 23:5–6).

Mark Lev, in his book *Lectures on Messianic Prophecy* (p. 125), commented on 2 Samuel 7:14, which reads, "I will be his father, and he shall be my son. If he commit iniquity, I will chasten him with the rod of men, and with the stripes of the children of men." Lev says, "This could be rendered, 'For iniquity committed [not by Him, but by men] I will chasten Him with the rod due to men, and with the stripes due to the children of men.'" This speaks of the vicarious sufferings of the Son of David and agrees with Isaiah 53:6. If the King James Version is correct, it is a reference to the backsliding and consequent chastening of Solomon, David's immediate successor.

The Lord not only made a promise to David, but He confirmed His promise by an oath: "The LORD hath sworn in truth unto David; he will not turn from it: Of the fruit of thy body will I set upon thy throne" (Ps. 132:11; cp. Heb. 6:13–18).

Again turning to the New Testament, we read: "The book of the genealogy of Jesus Christ, the son of David" (Mt. 1:11); and "Concerning his Son, Jesus Christ our Lord, who was made of the seed of David according to the flesh" (Rom. 1:3; cp. Lk. 1:30–35; Acts 2:29–30; 2 Tim. 2:8; Rev. 5:5; 22:16).

The public knew Jesus as the "Son of David" and so called Him (see Mt. 9:27; 12:22–23; 15:22; 20:30–31; 21:9, 15; Mk. 10:47–48; Lk. 18:38–39). The Pharisees also knew full well that the Messiah must be the Son of David. When Jesus asked them, "What think ye of Christ [Messiah]? Whose son is he? They say unto him, The Son of David" (Mt. 22:41–42). It is obvious that the Messiah had to be a son of David according to the flesh—and Jesus was.

During Bible times, every Jewish person could trace his genealogy. "So all Israel was reckoned by genealogies" (1 Chr. 9:1). These records were kept in the cities (Neh. 7:5–6; Ezra 2:1) and were public property. Each Israelite's genealogical record constitutes his title to his farm or home; therefore, he had a pecuniary interest in preserving the genealogical records of his family. These national genealogical records were carefully kept until the destruction of Jerusalem, the Temple and the Jewish state in A.D. 70. During the life of Jesus, no one offered to dispute the well-known fact that He was of the house and lineage of David, because it was in the public records to which all had access.

Since A.D. 70, when Israel's genealogical records (except those in the Bible) were destroyed or confused, no pretending Messiah can prove he is the son of David as prophecy demands. In other words, Messiah *had to come before A.D. 70.*

Of all of David's "many sons," the Messiah had to obtain His right to the throne of David through the regal line of *Solomon.*

And of all my sons (for the LORD hath given me many sons) he hath chosen Solomon, my son, to sit upon the throne of the kingdom of the LORD over Israel (1 Chr. 28:5; cp. v. 6; 1 Chr. 29:24).

In the New Testament, Solomon is in the royal line from David to Joseph (see Mt. 1:6).

Yet another most important *credential* for the Messiah is that *He had to be born of a virgin.* Since the Messiah had to be of the fruit of David's body (Ps. 132:11), this virgin had to be a *direct* descendant of King David.

Hear ye now, O house of David . . . the LORD himself shall give you a sign [a *sign* in the Bible is a *wonder,* a *miracle*]; *Behold, the virgin shall conceive, and bear a son, and shall call his name Immanuel* [God with us] (Isa. 7:13–14).

The New Revised Standard Version of the Bible is grossly in error in translating the Hebrew word *almah* in Isaiah 7:14 as "young woman."

Almah refers to a virgin in every instance of its use in the Old Testament (one of which is in Exodus 2:8, where it is used of a maid, a young girl, the baby Moses' sister). In the Septuagint, *almah* is translated as *parthenos*, the Greek word for virgin.

Indeed, whenever the birth of the Messiah is spoken of in the Old Testament, mention is made of His mother or the womb, but never of a human father. Consider the following references: "Thou art he who took me out of the *womb*" (Ps. 22:9); "The LORD hath called me from the *womb*" (Isa. 49:1); "And now, saith the LORD who formed me from the *womb* to be his servant" (Isa. 49:5); "The LORD hath created a new thing in the earth, A *woman* shall compass a man" (Jer. 31:22); "until the time that *she* who travaileth hath brought forth" (Mic. 5:3).

In the New Testament it is written that Jesus was indeed born of a virgin, a virgin who was a direct descendant of King David. After listing the genealogical record from Abraham to Christ, using the often repeated word "begat" to show descent by natural generation, we finally come to this striking statement:

Now the birth of Jesus Christ was in this way: When, as his mother, Mary, was espoused to Joseph, before they came together, she was found with child of the Holy Spirit . . . for that which is conceived in her is of the Holy Spirit. And she shall bring forth a son, and thou shalt call his name JESUS; for he shall save his people from their sins. Now all this was done, that it might be fulfilled which was spoken by the Lord through the prophet, saying, Behold, the virgin shall be with child, and shall bring forth a son, and they shall call his name Immanuel, which, being interpreted, is God with us (Mt. 1:18, 20–23).

This much is patently clear, whoever the Almighty sent to earth via the virgin birth is the Messiah; for here is a true "sign," a wonder of heavenly origin that cannot be counterfeited. The God who gave the specification in Isaiah 7:14 fulfilled it in the virgin birth of Jesus.

This messianic chain giving the Messiah's lineage was formed through many centuries: from Eve, to David, to Isaiah, to the Prophet Micah's time. It was added to by many human agents who spoke "in diverse manners, times and places" (A. T. Pierson, *God's Living Oracles*). And every time prophecy made a particular choice, there was a new risk, humanly speaking, of selecting the wrong branch; but nothing short of *absolute accuracy* will do when God speaks.

Absolute accuracy it was, for when the Messiah came He fulfilled to the letter all the specifications of His lineage. He was indeed the *seed of the*

woman, the *Son of Abraham*, the *Son of David* (Mt. 1:1). No other person in
the history of the world could have met all of these qualifications.

It is easy to see that if enough characteristic details are given, identification of the Messiah is positive. The same is true of prophecy. If a sufficient number of details are given, *identification is positive*. Many details
concerning the Messiah are given, and each one is exactly fulfilled in
Jesus of Nazareth, so that His identification is positive.

Moreover, prophecy has given us a further specific *credential*, His
address in terms of the town where He was to be born.

*But thou, Bethlehem Ephrathah, though thou be little among the
thousands of Judah, yet out of thee shall he come forth unto me that is
to be ruler in Israel, whose goings forth have been from of old, from
everlasting* (Mic. 5:2).

Of all the continents on earth, one was chosen—Asia; of all the states
of Asia, one was chosen—Canaan; of all the provinces of Palestine, one
was chosen—Judea; of all the cities of Judea, one was chosen—Bethlehem
Ephrathah, a tiny village having, at that time, fewer than one thousand
inhabitants. The prophet pinpointed one obscure village on the map of
the world, but he spoke infallibly, for the omniscient God was behind his
utterance. The prophet spoke clearly, with unequivocal certainty; for
when King Herod demanded of the chief priests and scribes of the people
where Christ should be born, they told him, "In Bethlehem of Judea, for
thus it is written by the prophet" (Mt. 2:4–6; cp. Jn. 7:42).

Jesus was born in Bethlehem of Judea (Mt. 2:1) in a manner altogether marvelous. Until shortly before the time of His birth, Mary was
living at the wrong place—wrong, that is, if her expected child was
indeed the Messiah. But, we cannot ignore the intricacies of God's
providence in fulfilling His Word. In 1923 at Ankara, Turkey, a Roman
temple inscription was found which, when deciphered, related that in
the reign of Caesar Augustus there were three great tax collections. The
second was ordered *four years before the birth of Christ*.

The proud Jewish people resented the idea of a special tax, so they
sent a commission to Rome to protest it. Quirinius, the local governor
of Syria, did not have the authority to settle the problem. Those were
days of slow communications and even slower travel. The commission
finally failed, and the Jewish people had to submit to the enrollment
and taxing. However, by the time the official tax collectors had worked
their way eastward, town by town and province by province, and after
the time-consuming delays caused by the Jewish protests, enough time

elapsed that, when the enrollment was put into force in Judea, *the exact time had come for the birth of the baby Jesus!*

Neither Mary, Caesar nor the Roman tax collectors controlled the timing, nor were they in charge of affairs. The God who rules the world behind the scenes had His hand on the wheel, and He literally moved the peoples of the world and timed everything to the very day, so that Mary and Joseph arrived in Bethlehem at the precise time, and Jesus, the Messiah, was born in the right place, the place designated by the infallible finger of prophecy!

Finally, to accurately identify the Messiah, the *time* of His coming was predicted.

First, the Messiah had to come *before the tribe of Judah lost its tribal identity: The scepter shall not depart from Judah, nor a lawgiver from between his feet, until Shiloh come; and unto him shall the gathering of the people be* (Gen. 49:10).

The word "scepter" in this passage does not necessarily refer to a king's staff. The primary meaning of the word translated "scepter" is a *tribal staff.* "The word *shebet*, which is translated 'scepter' in the Authorized Version signifies a rod or staff, particularly the rod or staff which belonged to each tribe as an ensign of their authority. Each tribe was in possession of its own peculiar 'rod' or 'staff' with its name inscribed thereon" (Bishop Sherlock, *Discourses on Prophecy*). Hence, the "scepter" signified their identity as a tribe. The *tribal identity* of Judah would not pass away—as did that of the other tribes of Israel—"until Shiloh come."

For ages, both Jewish and Christian commentators have taken "Shiloh" to be a name of Messiah. It means *peace* or *one sent.*

Even though the tribe of Judah, during the seventy-year period of their captivity in Babylon, had been deprived of national sovereignty, they *never lost their tribal staff, their national identity;* and they always had their own lawgivers (judges), even in captivity (Ezra 1:5, 8).

At the time of Christ, although the Romans were overlords of the Jews, the Jews had a king in their own land. Moreover, they were, to a large extent, governed by their own laws, and the Sanhedrin of the nation exercised its authority. But in the span of a few years (during the year when Jesus was twelve years of age and appeared publicly in the Temple, Lk. 2:41–52), Archelaus, the king of the Jews, was dethroned and banished. Coponius was appointed Roman Procurator, and the kingdom of Judah, the last remnant of the former greatness of the nation of Israel, was formally debased into a part of the province of Syria (see Josephus' *Antiquities* 17, chapter 13:1–5). For almost another half century, the Jewish people retained the semblance of a provincial governmental structure; but in A.D. 70, both their city and Temple were destroyed by the armies of the Roman General Titus, and all semblance of Jewish national sovereignty disappeared. The remarkable thing is that the Messiah (Shiloh) came *before* Judah lost its tribal identity, exactly as stated in Genesis 49:10!

Twenty-two years before the Lord Jesus was crucified, the Sanhedrin lost the power of passing the death sentence (see Jn. 18:31) when Judah became a Roman province. Rabbi Rachmon said, "When the members of the Sanhedrin found themselves deprived of their right over life and death, a general consternation took possession of them; they covered their heads with ashes and their bodies with sackcloth, exclaiming, 'Woe unto us, for the scepter has departed from Judah and the Messiah has not come'" (*Chosen People*). The rabbis did not realize that the Messiah had come. From this it is apparent that they considered Genesis 49:10 a messianic passage and had a clear concept of its meaning.

Second, the Messiah had to come *while the second Temple was still standing.* *And I will shake all nations, and the desire of all nations shall come; and I will fill this house with glory, saith the LORD of hosts . . . The glory of this latter house shall be greater than of the former, saith the LORD of hosts; and in this place will I give peace, saith the LORD of hosts* (Hab. 2:7, 9).

Malachi confirmed Haggai's prophecy, "the Lord, whom ye seek, shall suddenly come to his temple" (Mal. 3:1). This prediction in Malachi, as well as the one in Haggai, could not be fulfilled *after* the destruction of the Temple in A.D. 70. Therefore, if the Messiah were to come, He had to come before the Temple was destroyed. Zechariah 11:13 also demands that the Messiah come before the destruction of the Jewish Temple, for that prediction speaks of "thirty pieces of silver" being "cast . . . unto the potter in the house of the LORD." In Psalm 118:26 the prophetic pen informs us that the people who would welcome the Messiah were to say not only, "Blessed is he that cometh in the name of the LORD," but also, "we have blessed you out of the house of the LORD." That is, from the house of the Lord (the Temple) the people would bless Him when He came.

All of this prophecy was beautifully fulfilled in the life of Jesus. When He approached Jerusalem for His triumphal entry, the people said, "Blessed is he that cometh in the name of the Lord! Hosanna in the highest!" (Mt. 21:9). We then read that Jesus healed many who were blind and lame *in the Temple* (Mt. 21:14), and there can be no doubt that those who were healed in the Temple blessed Him in the house of the Lord, even as Psalm 118:26 predicted they would!

There is another specific fulfillment to this prophecy. Matthew 21:15 informs us that the children cried out *in the Temple*, saying, "Hosanna to the Son of David!" Surely, "Out of the mouth of babes and sucklings thou hast perfected praise" (Mt. 21:16; cp. Ps. 8:2). God used *children* to fulfill His prediction given in Psalm 118:26 that the Messiah would be blessed in the house of the Lord!

Thus, at least five scriptural predictions of the coming of the Messiah *demand that He come while the Temple at Jerusalem was still standing.* This is of great significance, inasmuch as the Temple has not been rebuilt since its destruction in A.D. 70. These five Scriptures are Psalm 118:26; Haggai 2:7, 9; Zechariah 11:13 and Malachi 3:1.

Clearly, the public entry of Jesus into Jerusalem and the Temple, as reported in the New Testament, was prearranged and predicted in the Old Testament (see Mt. 21:1–16; Mk. 11:1–11; Lk. 19:29–40).

And Jesus went into the temple of God . . . And the blind and the lame came to him in the temple, and he healed them . . . and the children crying in the temple, and saying, Hosanna to the Son of David! (Mt. 21:12–15).

Two other Scriptures bear on this: when the child Jesus was taken to the Temple by His parents, as recorded in Luke 2:25–32; and when Jesus, as a boy of twelve, was "in the temple, sitting in the midst of the teachers . . . And all that heard him were amazed at his understanding"(Lk. 2:46–47).

After years, even centuries, of waiting, the Messiah suddenly came to His Temple (Mal. 3:1)! A few years later, God destroyed the Temple and the city of Jerusalem, even as Jesus had warned. Clearly, the Messiah has already come. He can't come now, since there is no Temple. The Messiah had to come almost 2,000 years ago, before God had the Temple destroyed.

Jesus warned that the Temple, the heart of Jewish worship, the very heart and soul of their national existence, would be torn down, and "There shall not be left here one stone upon another" (Mt. 24:2). As Jesus, the true Prophet, said, so it came to pass—no doubt sooner that the disciples expected.

Third, Daniel said something very remarkable about the coming of Christ relative to the Temple. In giving the timetable from his time to the coming of the Messiah, Daniel made it clear that the Messiah would come and be "cut off" (die) before the "people [the Romans] of the prince that shall come shall destroy the city [Jerusalem] and the sanctuary [the Temple]" (Dan. 9:26).

Fourth, the Messiah had to come *483 years after a specific date in Daniel's time.* This definite prediction as to the exact time of the coming of the Messiah is one of the most wonderful prophecies in the entire Bible. It established the date of the Messiah's advent almost 500 years before He came.

> *Know, therefore, and understand, that from the going forth of the commandment to restore and to build Jerusalem unto the Messiah, the Prince, shall be seven weeks, and threescore and two weeks; the street shall be built again, and the wall, even in troublous times. And after threescore and two weeks shall Messiah be cut off, but not for himself; and the people of the prince that shall come shall destroy the city and the sanctuary* (Dan. 9:25–26).

The date of the "commandment to restore and to build Jerusalem" was the decree by Artaxerxes in 444 B.C. granting permission to the Jews to return to Palestine and rebuild the city of Jerusalem (see Neh. 2:1–8).

The Hebrew word translated "weeks" in Daniel 9:25–26 means *sevens* and is used for years (see Gen. 29:27–28; Lev. 25:8). In other words, the *seventy sevens* which are prophetically determined on Israel and the holy city with specified events (v. 24) is a *period of 490 years.* This period is divided into three sections: (1) Seven "weeks," or seven sevens of years—the 49 years the prophet allotted for the rebuilding of Jerusalem under the leadership of Nehemiah and Ezra and their associates (see the Books of Ezra and Nehemiah). History tells us it took 49 years to do this rebuilding job. (2) A second period of 62 "weeks," or 434 years, to the time of the Messiah. (3) The 70th "week," or a period of seven years sometime after the coming of the Messiah.

The period "from . . . the commandment to restore and to build Jerusalem unto Messiah, the Prince, is a period of 483 years. Sir Robert Anderson in his book, *The Coming Prince,* made some calculations and gave the world his findings.

He begins with March 14, 444 B.C., the date of "the commandment to restore and to build Jerusalem"; and he ends the period with Jesus' triumphal entry into Jerusalem, which he believes was the official presentation of the Messiah as "Prince" to Israel (cp. Lk. 19:38; Zech 9:9). After careful investigation and consultation with noted astronomers, he gives these startling findings. From 444 B.C. to A.D. 32 is 476 years; 476 multiplied by 365 is 173,740 days; from March 14 to April 6 (the day of Christ's triumphal entry) is 24 days; add 116 days for leap years, and the total is 173,880 days. Since the *prophetic year* of the Bible is always 360 days, the 69 *sevens* of the prophecy in Daniel (69 multiplied by 7, multiplied by 360) equals 173,880 days. And so, the time given by Daniel from the "commandment to restore and to build Jerusalem unto the Messiah, the Prince" works out perfectly— to the very day!

This is a prophecy as detailed as a road map with not a taint of uncertainty. It is a prediction which can be conclusively proven. It points unerringly to Jesus of Nazareth who was "Messiah, the Prince" who was "cut off" by a violent death, "but not for himself." When Jesus began His public ministry, He said significantly, "The time is fulfilled, and the kingdom of God is at hand" (Mk. 1:15). Thus, with absolute certainty the exact year, the very month of a notable event in His life was foretold.

These twelve elements comprise the Messiah's credentials. They were given in the prophetic Word so that all might know the Messiah when He came. The accuracy of these predictions is minute; the fulfillments are exact. All is in perfect agreement: *Jesus of Nazareth fulfills all the specifications* foretold as to His lineage, His birthplace and the time of His birth. It is a nondebatable fact that within a generation of Christ's sufferings on the cross, the Temple was destroyed, the Jewish priesthood ceased to exist, the sacrifices were no longer offered, the Jewish genealogical records were destroyed, the Jewish people's holy city was destroyed, and the people of Israel were driven out of their land, sold into slavery and dispersed to the four corners of the earth!

Prophecies Concerning the Life and Ministry of the Messiah

The Messiah's Character and Characteristics are Clearly Delineated: He Will be the Sinless One, as Holy as God

The Messiah must be as righteous as God himself, for He will be the "righteous Branch . . . he shall be called, THE LORD OUR RIGHTEOUSNESS " (Jer. 23:5–6). The Messiah must be God's chosen One in whom He "delighteth" (Isa. 42:1). In Matthew 3:17 the Father says of Jesus, "This is my beloved Son, in whom I am well pleased." The Messiah, on His part, will be the obedient *servant of the Lord* who will ever "delight to do thy [God's] will" (Ps. 40:8). The Lord Jesus could testify, "My food is to do the will of him that sent me, and to finish his work" (Jn. 4:34; cp. Jn. 6:38).

The Messiah will be anointed by the Holy Spirit in a manner and degree far beyond any other man ("above" His "fellows," Ps. 45:7; cp. Heb. 1:9). Another remarkable passage, Isaiah 11:2–5, tells us:

And the Spirit of the LORD shall rest upon him, the spirit of wisdom and understanding, the spirit of counsel and might, the spirit of knowledge and of the fear of the LORD, And shall make him of quick understanding in the fear of the LORD; and he shall not judge after the sight of his eyes, neither reprove after the hearing of his ears, But with righteousness shall

*he judge the poor . . . And righteousness shall be the girdle of his loins,
and faithfulness the girdle of his waist.*

In the New Testament, we read of Jesus' anointing with the Holy
Spirit at the time of His baptism when the Holy Spirit descended like a
dove and sat upon Him (Mt. 3:16). He bore witness that the "Spirit of
the Lord" was upon Him (Lk. 4:18), which was in fulfillment of a prediction about the Messiah's character and ministry in Isaiah 61:1–3. The
people "bore him [Jesus] witness, and wondered at the gracious words
which proceeded out of his mouth (Lk. 4:22).

The Messiah must be a man of perfect self-control, "He shall not cry,
nor lift up, nor cause his voice [in anger or as an excited rabble-rouser]
to be heard in the street" (Isa. 42:2). He will have patience with the frail-
ties of men, "A bruised reed shall he not break, and smoking flax shall
he not quench" (Isa. 42:3). The Messiah will have perseverance in the
course of doing His Father's will. He will have courage and success in
that goal, as well as steadfastness of purpose, "He shall not fail nor be
discouraged" (Isa. 42:4). Matthew, in describing the ministry of Jesus,
said that He fulfilled what Isaiah had said about Him:

*That it might be fulfilled which was spoken by Isaiah, the prophet, say-
ing, Behold my servant, whom I have chosen; my beloved, in whom my
soul is well pleased; I will put my Spirit upon him, and he shall show
justice to the Gentiles. He shall not strive, nor cry; neither shall any man
hear his voice in the streets. A bruised reed shall he not break, and smoking flax shall he not quench, till he send forth justice unto victory. And
in his name shall the Gentiles trust* (Mt. 12:17–21).

The Messiah's compassion and tenderness are revealed in an exquisite
figure of touching tenderness, "He shall feed his flock like a shepherd; he
shall gather the lambs with his arm, and carry them in his bosom, and
shall gently lead those that are with young" (Isa. 40:11). In the New
Testament, we read of the compassion of Jesus in Matthew 9:36; 14:14;
15:32 and many other places. In the tenth chapter of John, Christ is presented as the "good shepherd" who loves His sheep and cares for them,
even to the point of giving His life for them (Jn. 10:11–18).

The Messiah will be "just" and "lowly" (Zech. 9:9); "fairer than the
children of men" with "grace . . . poured into thy lips" and blessed by
God forever (Ps. 45:2). He will be without "violence," indicating a
blameless outward life; "neither was any deceit in his mouth," indicating an innocent inner life (Isa. 53:9; cp. 1 Pet. 2:22). He will suffer great
personal wrong done to Him without complaining to God or man (Isa.

53:7; 50:6–7). In the New Testament, we learn that Jesus was "meek and lowly in heart" (Mt. 11:29); and the Father testified of Him, "Thou hast loved righteousness, and hated iniquity; therefore, God . . . hath anointed thee with the oil of gladness above thy fellows" (Heb. 1:9). When the Lord Jesus was crucified, He meekly suffered all the indignities, insults, blasphemies, mental torture and physical violence heaped upon Him and did not complain; in fact, He prayed for His persecutors (Mt. 27:12–14; Lk. 23:34).

As a teacher, the Messiah "shall not fail . . . till he have set justice in the earth," and the nations "shall wait for his law" (Isa. 42:4). Today, multitudes in our most advanced nations wait on Jesus' teaching; and when the Kingdom of God, with Christ as King, is finally set up on earth, He will indeed have "set justice in the earth."

The word "justice" is a very rich word, translated by 31 different words in the King James Version. It means to bring *law, order, salvation, truth and righteousness* to mankind. The Messiah's ministry was to bring salvation and truth (justice) to Jews and Gentiles alike (Isa. 42:6).

It was prewritten of the Messiah that He would "open [His] mouth in a parable," He will "utter dark sayings of old" (Ps. 78:2). When Jesus the great Teacher came, He taught "as one having authority, and not as the scribes" (Mt. 7:29). The scribes taught by quoting what certain rabbis had said; but when Jesus taught, He gave God's words and spoke with finality and assurance, "Verily, verily, I say unto you . . ."(Jn. 5:24; 6:47; etc.). Moreover, Christ's characteristic method of teaching was by the use of parables: "and without a parable spoke he not unto them, That it might be fulfilled which was spoken by the prophet, saying, I will open my mouth in parables" (Mt. 13:34–35).

It is clear in the Old Testament that when the Messiah comes, He will be holier and wiser than men, even as just and righteous as God himself.

The Portrayal of the Perfect Character

As was foretold throughout the Old Testament Scriptures, when the Messiah did come, He possessed the perfect character. He was Jesus the Christ. That which is given in general terms and in an abstract way in the Old Testament, in portraying the coming perfect Messiah, became a concrete reality, in the flesh, in the person of Jesus Christ in the New Testament. In the Lord Jesus we see the One who is altogether lovely, the chief among ten thousand, the delight of the Heavenly Father.

Christ's perfectly poised character was not unbalanced by eccentricities or human foibles. His perfections were not tainted by pride, nor was His wisdom marred by an occasional bit of folly. His equity was not twisted by prejudice, nor was His justice adulterated by selfish whims. He had a becoming dignity which was happily blended with His gracious humility. He had concern for others without worry, zeal without fretfulness, patience without dilatoriness, tact without dishonesty, and frankness without rudeness. His authority was balanced and blended with gentleness and patience.

He never had to admit defeat, retract a statement, offer an apology, change His teachings, confess a sin or a mistake, or ask advice. He never lost His temper or spoke rashly. He was never bested in an argument; He always had the right answer—the will and Word of God.

He went about doing good, prayed much, gave God the glory and thanks in all things, and had no interest in the accumulation of material things. He lived and died in poverty, yet He never lacked until His time of suffering on the cross.

His miracles were all beneficent, never for vainglory. He was the perfect Teacher and lived what He taught. He was, in the truest sense, the Son of man; yet He was not one of us, for He never sinned. He was from above and not from the earth, and He was the unique Son of God. No other man was like this man.

He never made a claim to supernatural power or prerogative without performing a miracle to prove it. He who said, "I am the light of the world" (Jn. 9:5) also opened the eyes of the man born blind, so that all could see His right to the claim. He who said, "I am the resurrection, and the life" (Jn. 11:25) proved that these were sober words of truth by raising Lazarus from the dead (Jn. 11:25, 43–44). He who said, "I am the bread of life" (Jn. 6:35) gave full evidence that He was all He claimed to be by performing the miracle of feeding the five thousand from five loaves and two fish (Jn. 6:5–14).

Volumes have been written, volumes more probably will be written, on the moral glory and perfect character of the Lord Jesus. In summation, suffice it to say that He is the image of the invisible God (Heb. 1:3), the sum and substance of all good, the One in whom dwelt all the fullness of the Godhead (Col. 2:9). His holiness shone with undiminished luster; His loveliness was as pure and genuine as the glory of God. His love was as selfless and complete as the love of God, for in all the history of the world, mankind has never seen, except in the death of Christ, a perfect character dying under an unparalleled weight of unmerited agony. The mighty yet lowly royal sufferer uncomplainingly bore the weight of the sin of all humanity in His atoning death on the cross.

The Messiah's Supernatural Miracles are Clearly Foretold

The Messiah must show as His hallmarks supernatural works which prove Him to be the God-appointed, God-sent Redeemer. As His *special* work, the Messiah would offer Himself as a substitutionary sacrifice to redeem the race. The Messiah's ministry must *bless* people, as Isaiah foretold:

The Spirit of the Lord GOD is upon me, because the LORD hath anointed me to preach good tidings unto the meek; he hath sent me to bind up the brokenhearted, to proclaim liberty to the captives, and the opening of the prison to those who are bound; To proclaim the acceptable year of the LORD . . . to give unto them beauty for ashes, the oil of joy for mourning, the garment of praise for the spirit of heaviness (Isa. 61:1–3).

The Messiah, as the Lord God in the midst of the people, must be the miracle worker par excellence.

Behold, your God will come . . . he will come and save you. Then the eyes of the blind shall be opened, and the ears of the deaf shall be unstopped. Then shall the lame man leap as an hart, and the tongue of the dumb sing (Isa. 35:4–6).

I, the LORD, have called thee in righteousness . . . and give thee for a covenant of the people, for a light of the nations, To open the blind eyes, to bring out the prisoners from the prison (Isa. 42:6–7).

The Messiah will be the worldwide Savior for "salvation unto the end of the earth" (Isa. 49:6), as a "light of the nations" (Isa. 42:6–7; 11:10) and the "Redeemer of Israel" (Isa. 49:7).

In the New Testament, Christ is revealed as the worldwide Savior, "For God so loved the world, that he gave his only begotten Son, that whosoever believeth in him should not perish, but have everlasting life" (Jn. 3:16).

The Prophet Simeon, when he saw the child Jesus in the Temple, knew that He was the Christ. He said, "Lord . . . mine eyes have seen thy salvation, Which thou hast prepared before the face of all people; A light to lighten the Gentiles, and the glory of thy people, Israel" (Lk. 2:29–32; cp. Lk. 1:68–79; Rom. 3:28–30; etc.).

The Messiah's *special* work would be to offer Himself, His soul and body, as a ransom, an offering, a supreme sacrifice of Himself. He will bruise Satan's head (Gen. 3:15; cp. Heb. 2:14; 1 Jn. 3:8); and by that great work of redemption, He will establish a kingdom that will last forever (Isa. 9:7; Dan. 7:14; Lk. 1:32–33; Heb. 2:9–14).

The identification of the Old Testament Messiah in the Christ of the New Testament is perfect, describing His holy character, miraculous works and sacrificial death on the cross. The miracles Jesus wrought were well-known by His generation. Peter, in his sermon on the day of Pentecost, used the reality of Christ's miracle-working ministry as *proof* of His Messiahship:

Ye men of Israel, hear these words: Jesus of Nazareth, a man approved of God among you by miracles and wonders and signs, which God did by him in the midst of you, as ye yourselves also know . . . Whom God hath raised up . . . let all the house of Israel know assuredly, that God hath made that same Jesus . . . both Lord and Christ (Acts 2:22, 24, 36).

In the Gospels, Jesus blessed, saved and helped all seekers who contacted Him. He healed the sick, cleansed the lepers, opened the eyes of the blind, raised the dead, fed the hungry, walked on the Sea of Galilee and performed many other miracles (see Mk. 1:32, 34, 41–42; Jn. 6:11–13, 19–21; 9:7; 11:43–44; etc.).

John the Baptist, after his imprisonment by King Herod, sent two of his disciples to Jesus to ask Him, "Art thou he that should come [the Messiah], or do we look for another?" (Mt. 11:2–3). In essence, he was asking, *Are you the Messiah or are you not?* Jesus answered by reminding John and his disciples of His *miracle works*, thus assuring them that He was the Messiah, for only the Messiah could do those works: "Go and show John again those things which ye do hear and see: The blind receive their sight, and the lame walk, and the lepers are cleansed, and the deaf hear, the dead are raised up, and the poor have the gospel preached to them" (Mt. 11:4–5). These miracles are the very marks of the Messiah given in the Old Testament!

Finally, after His benevolent ministry of healing and blessing the people, Christ accomplished the great work for which He came into the world, the work to which He was foreordained from before the foundation of the world (see 1 Pet. 1:18–20). He died on the cross, offering Himself as a vicarious sacrifice to redeem the race: "Christ Jesus, Who gave himself a ransom for all" (1 Tim. 2:5–6); "Jesus . . . by the grace of God, should taste death for every man" (Heb. 2:9); "once, in the end of the ages, hath he [Christ] appeared to put away sin by the sacrifice of himself" (Heb. 9:26).

Jesus himself appealed to the people to believe on Him for the sake of the miracles He had performed:

Believest thou not that I am in the Father, and the Father in me? The words that I speak unto you, I speak not of myself; but the Father that dwelleth in me, he doeth the works. Believe me that I am in the Father, and the Father in me; or else believe me for the very works' sake (Jn. 14:10–11).

Indeed, Jesus had this *triple seal* as proof of his genuineness: (1) a perfect character; (2) miracle works; (3) Himself as a sacrifice for the redemption of all mankind. These three requirements clearly establish the fact that Jesus is the true Messiah, for He fulfilled all three!

During the last 2,000 years, His gospel has literally been preached around the world, and millions of Gentiles, as well as multitudes of Jewish people, have trusted and are trusting Him. Jesus is indeed the universal Savior, the "Lamb of God, who taketh away the sin of the world" (Jn. 1:29). His love envelopes the world (Jn. 3:16); His gospel is for every creature (Mk. 16:15); His is the only "name under heaven given among men, whereby we must be saved" (Acts 4:12).

Prophecies Concerning
the Prophetic Paradoxes

The Old Testament presents a mysterious prophetic puzzle of strange combinations of prophecies concerning the coming Messiah which appear at times so conflicting that they seem impossible to fulfill. These seemingly contradictory and apparently irreconcilable prophecies are called *prophetic paradoxes*. A *prophetic paradox* is made up of two or more prophecies each of which contains a *seeming contradiction* with no real absurdity involved and presenting an enigma which, without a clue to its fulfillment, seems impossible to solve. The Old Testament abounds with such prophetic paradoxes concerning the Messiah which were and still are absolute mysteries except as the New Testament solves them in Christ.

This amazing feature of many messianic predictions prevents both wicked men and overzealous disciples from purposely fulfilling them, if they could; for the prophecies, in at least some instances, were not fully understood until the fulfillment explained and made them clear (see 1 Pet. 1:10–11). Such unique prophecies absolutely prove that the God of prophecy, who designed them, and the God of providence, who fulfilled them, are one.

Another astonishing feature about these prophetic paradoxes is the perfectly normal, artless way in which they were providentially, even miraculously, fulfilled in the life of Jesus Christ in the New Testament. It is not necessary to strain or force either the facts or the predictions to make them conform.

Consider some of these *impossible* contrasts: God will come to earth to be born as a child. The Messiah will be begotten by God, yet He will be God. He will be "a son" in time, yet He is "The Everlasting Father" (Isa. 9:6). Chosen by God, elect, precious, yet despised and rejected by men, He is a "man of sorrows, and acquainted with grief" (Isa. 53:3). Coming to the Jewish people and being rejected by them as a nation, He will be sought by the Gentiles and will be a "light to the nations" (Isa. 49:6). He will be a man who is God, and God who is man. Sinless and having a wholly benevolent ministry, He will eventually be forsaken by both God and man. He will be abhorred, yet extolled and exalted; "cut off," yet His days will be prolonged. "Grief and glory, travail and triumph, humiliation and exaltation, cross and crown are so strongly intermingled that the ancient Jewish expositors could not reconcile these prophecies. The whole prophetic picture of the coming Messiah, with its fulfillment, is so wholly novel, so mysterious, so artless and yet so intricate, that it was and is and must forever remain the wonder of all literature" (A. T. Pierson).

Consider these few of the many prophetic paradoxes in the predictions of the coming Messiah.

The Messiah's Birth

Notice in the following predictions these striking irreconcilables: A virgin is to bear a son, something unknown in human experience. And, this child will be God, "God with us." He will be God-begotten and yet God incarnate!

Therefore the Lord himself shall give you a sign; Behold, the virgin shall conceive, and bear a son, and shall call his name Immanuel (Isa. 7:14).

For unto us a child is born, unto us a son is given, and the government shall be upon his shoulder; and his name shall be called Wonderful, Counselor, The Mighty God, The Everlasting Father, The Prince of Peace (Isa. 9:6).

To fulfill these amazing prophecies, God performed a *biological miracle*; Christ was conceived by the Holy Spirit (Lk. 1:35) and born of the virgin Mary, as recorded in Matthew 1:16–25. To fulfill these two predictions made 700 years before, God in the person of His Son came to earth, and the incarnation became a reality; "the Son of the Highest"

(Lk. 1:32) became Mary's son, God manifest in the flesh (see Lk. 1:31–33; Jn. 1:1–3, 14; 1 Tim. 3:16)—and all of this although Mary knew not a man (Lk. 1:34).

Not only was the Messiah to be the God-Man, born of a virgin (Isa. 7:14; 9:6), but He was, in some mysterious way, to be all of the following as well: the seed of the woman (Gen. 3:15); "the Son of man" (Dan. 7:13); the Son of God (Ps. 2:7); the seed of Abraham (Gen. 22:18); and the "fruit" of David's body (Ps. 132:11). But how could God be a man and man be God and, at the same time, be a son of man and Son of God? How can a person be God and yet be born of God? How can one be a "Son of man" and yet have no human father? How can He be the seed of the woman when the woman knew not a man? How could one person be all of these? Wonder of wonders, Jesus was! The Lord Jesus was God (Jn. 1:1); He was man (Jn. 1:14); He was the seed of the woman (Gal. 4:4); He was the Son of man, the representative man (Lk. 19:10); He was the Son of God (Jn. 3:16); He was the seed of Abraham and the seed of David (Mt. 1:1). Here, then, we have the miracle of the ages: Christ Jesus, perfect man, yet very God; God-begotten, yet God incarnate in one indivisible, loving, matchless personality. The Apostle John explained the supreme mystery (called the "mystery of God . . . and of Christ," Col. 2:2; 4:3) in these words:

In the beginning was the Word, and the Word was with God, and the Word was God. The same was in the beginning with God . . . And the Word was made flesh, and dwelt among us (and we beheld his glory, the glory as of the only begotten of the Father), full of grace and truth . . . the only begotten Son, who is in the bosom of the Father (Jn. 1:1–2, 14, 18).

The Messiah's Place of Origin

From where did He come? Bethlehem? Egypt? Nazareth? Here is another involved series of predictions. Prophecy said, "But thou, Bethlehem Ephrathah . . . out of thee shall he come forth . . . that is to be ruler in Israel" (Mic. 5:2). But another Scripture said, "I . . . called my son out of Egypt" (Hos. 11:1). And there was a spoken prophecy commonly known among the people of Israel as one of the predictions of the prophets, "He shall be called a Nazarene" (Mt. 2:23), possibly based on Isaiah 11:1 where the Messiah is called the "Branch" (Heb., *neh-tzer*), meaning the *separated One* or *the Nazarene*.

Are these contradictions? Not at all, after the person came who unlocked the puzzle by the course of events in His divinely ordained life.

He was *born in Bethlehem,* as Micah said. Soon after His birth, He was *taken* to Egypt by Joseph and Mary, and from there God called Him back to Palestine following the death of wicked King Herod (Mt. 2:13–23). When Joseph and Mary returned to Palestine with the child Jesus, they *lived in Nazareth,* the city where the Lord was reared; hence, in His ministry He was called "Jesus of Nazareth" (Lk. 18:37; Acts 2:22; etc.).

There is an interesting historical sidelight that adds pungency to the understanding of these predictions and their fulfillments. When Joseph and Mary returned from Egypt, Joseph was apparently about to settle near Bethlehem in Judea:

> But when he heard that Archelaus did reign in Judea in the place of his father, Herod, he was afraid to go there . . . he turned aside into the parts of Galilee; And he came and dwelt in a city called Nazareth, that it might be fulfilled which was spoken by the prophets, He shall be called a Nazarene (Mt. 2:22–23).

Humanly speaking, everything hinged on one peculiar fact: In a peevish fret before his death, King Herod changed his will and appointed Archelaus, the most wicked of his living sons, to rule instead of Antipas. It was this fear of Archelaus that led Joseph to look for another residence; then God led him to Nazareth. And so, God, who uses the wrath of man to praise Him, permitted the wrath of a petulant king to bring to pass a fulfillment of His Word (see Ps. 76:10).

Being of the tribe of Judah and being born in Bethlehem, Jesus was indeed a true "Nazarene," a "separated one," by living in Galilee instead of with his Judean brethren in the land of Judah. Joseph of old also was separated (*nazared*) from his brethren by his exile for so many years in Egypt (see Gen. 49:26, where the word *separate* comes from the Hebrew root *nazar*).

The historical record of the life of Jesus completely resolves these three seemingly contradictory prophecies.

How Could the Messiah be Both David's Son and David's Lord?

Christ himself raised this interesting question with the Pharisees when He asked them pointedly:

> What think ye of Christ? Whose son is he? They say unto him, The Son of David. He saith unto them, How, then, doth David, in the Spirit, call him Lord, saying, The LORD said unto my Lord, Sit thou on my right hand, till I make thine enemies thy footstool? If David, then, call him Lord, how is he his son? (Mt. 22:42–45; cp. Ps. 110:1).

It is not hard to see how Christ could be both David's son and David's Lord when we have the key to the situation in the facts as presented in the New Testament. Christ was David's son in that He was a descendant of David after the flesh (Lk. 1:32; Rom. 1:3); and He was David's Lord, for the Messiah is God, "KING OF KINGS, AND LORD OF LORDS" (Rev. 19:16). The Messiah is called "LORD" (Jehovah) in Jeremiah 23:6, "God" (Elohim) in Psalm 45:6 (cp. Heb. 1:8) and "Lord" (Adonai) in Psalm 110:1 and Malachi 3:1. All three are names and titles of deity in the Old Testament. It is clear that the Messiah is not only David's Lord, but He is *Lord of all*.

The Messiah's Right to David's Throne

Here we encounter an intricate, involved puzzle. Christ, the seed of David, must be virgin born and yet have a legal right to the throne of David, despite the fact that one of Solomon's descendants was an evil man named Jeconiah, of whom it was written, "Is this man Coniah [Jeconiah] a despised broken idol? Is he a vessel in which is no pleasure? Why are they cast out, he and his seed, and are cast into a land which they knew not? . . . Thus saith the LORD, Write this man childless, a man that shall not prosper in his days; for no man of his seed shall prosper, sitting upon the throne of David, and ruling any more in Judah" (Jer. 22:28, 30). Despite the fact that in Israel, *the right to the throne was transmitted only through the male line*, Christ was born of a virgin.

It is patently clear that the Messiah would inherit "the throne of David" (1 Chr. 17:11, 14; Ps. 132:11; Isa. 9:7; Jer. 33:15–17). But since He had to be born of a virgin, *how would He obtain His legal right to the throne of David?* How could the roadblock erected by Jeconiah's sin be circumvented? Who could untangle these predictions which seem hopelessly confused. The Master who devised the strange prophecies also worked out their fulfillment. The Prophet Isaiah said, "The zeal of the LORD of hosts will perform this" (Isa. 9:7).

Not only was the apparently impossible paradox resolved in Jesus the Christ, but God has given us the complete record of how He did it in the genealogies of the New Testament. Matthew records the genealogy of Christ through *Joseph*. This genealogy shows Christ to be the son of David (giving Him the right to David's throne) and also the son of Abraham (giving Him the right to the land of promise, the territorial possessions given to Abraham and his seed).

Luke traces the genealogy of Christ through Heli (Mary's father) back to Adam and God (Lk. 3:23–38), giving Christ a title deed to the whole earth as the son of Adam (see Gen. 1:27–30; Ps. 8:4–6; Heb. 2:6–9; Rev. 5:1–10) and to "all things" as the Son of God (see Heb. 1:2).

In Matthew's genealogy, Joseph is seen to be in the *regal* line of descent from King David down through *Solomon*. But Joseph was also a descendant of David through Jeconiah; hence, succession to the throne for Joseph personally is barred. Matthew's genealogical record is careful to show that Jesus was *not*, through Joseph, the fruit of David's body (i.e., a direct descendant of David through Joseph).

Luke gives Christ's genealogy through Mary. Heli was obviously Mary's father, Joseph's father-in-law (Lk. 3:23).

It is interesting to note that in the genealogical record of Matthew, it is written that "Jacob begat Joseph" (Mt. 1:16); that is, Jacob was the actual father of Joseph. In Luke, however, it is written that "Joseph . . . was the son of Heli" (Lk. 3:23). The word "son" is not in the original but was supplied by the translators. The verse should read, "son-in-law" instead of "son." Obviously, Joseph could not have had two fathers; hence, he is the son-in-law of Heli, his son in the sense that he married Heli's daughter. This is in accordance with Jewish custom (see 1 Sam. 24:16).

Christ is shown to be the *literal* fruit of David's body through His mother Mary. But (and this is important), while Mary was in a *royal* line from David, she was *not* in the *regal* lineage, for she was a descendant of King David through *Nathan*; whereas the right to the throne came through *Solomon* (see 1 Chr. 28:5–6). Therefore, Joseph's marriage to Mary *before Christ was born* was an absolute necessity, and that is exactly what occurred!

> *Now the birth of Jesus Christ was in this way: When, as his mother, Mary, was espoused to Joseph, before they came together, she was found with child of the Holy Spirit . . . behold, an angel of the Lord appeared unto him [Joseph] in a dream, saying, Joseph, thou son of David, fear not to take unto thee Mary, thy wife; for that which is conceived in her is of the Holy Spirit* (Mt. 1:18, 20).

The importance of the genealogical records in the Bible should not be minimized, because they are of prime importance in proving that Jesus is the Messiah and that He has a right to the throne of David. The genealogical records in the New Testament show the importance God places on the *proof* that Jesus is David's son and indirectly show the importance of the entire argument from fulfilled prophecy.

And so, through Mary, Jesus obtained His *literal* descent from King David; and from Mary's marriage to Joseph, who was also a son of David, He obtained His *legal* right to David's throne, for Mary was Joseph's wife *before Jesus was born*, making Joseph His legal father (foster father). Additionally, the prophecy concerning Jeconiah was fulfilled as well, for Jesus is *not* the seed (a direct descendant) of Jeconiah.

The Messiah Was to be Both the Chief Cornerstone and a Stone of Stumbling or Rock of Offense

He shall be . . . for a stone of stumbling and for a rock of offense to both the houses of Israel (Isa. 8:14).

The stone which the builders refused is become the head of the corner (Ps. 118:22; cp. Isa. 28:16).

To unbelievers, the Messiah would be a "rock of offense" and a "stone of stumbling." Peter explained the mystery by showing that everything depends on a person's attitude toward Christ, whether of faith or unbelief:

Wherefore also it is contained in the scripture, Behold, I lay in Zion a chief cornerstone, elect, precious; and he that believeth on him shall not be confounded. Unto you, therefore, who believe he is precious, but unto them who are disobedient, the stone which the builders disallowed, the same is made the head of the corner, And a stone of stumbling, and a rock of offense, even to them who stumble at the word, being disobedient (1 Pet. 2:6–8; cp. Rom. 9:32–33).

As He did so often, the Lord Jesus called attention to the prophecy in the Old Testament, showing Himself to be the New Testament fulfillment of it: "Jesus saith unto them, Did ye never read in the scriptures, The stone which the builders rejected, the same is become the head of the corner; this is the Lord's doing, and it is marvelous in our eyes?" (Mt. 21:42). The Lord also added this significant statement: "And whosoever shall fall on this stone [seeking His mercy and grace] shall be broken [his hopes in himself completely crushed], but on whomsoever it shall fall [in judgment], it will grind him to powder [completely ruin him for time and eternity]" (Mt. 21:44).

To the believer, Christ is the *Chief Cornerstone*, and He is very precious. To the unbeliever, Christ is the *Stone of Stumbling* or *Rock of Offense*. To the one, Christ brings eternal salvation; to the other, He brings judgment. Those who stumble in unbelief over Christ reject Him and fall to their eternal destruction.

The Messiah Was to be Rejected by Israel Yet Become a Light to the Nations and Salvation to the Ends of the Earth

Racially, the Messiah would be a Jew, a "rod out of the stem of Jesse
. . . a root of Jesse" (Isa. 11:1, 10); and yet the Gentiles would seek Him
(Isa. 11:10), an unheard of thing, for there is and has been through the
ages animosity between Jews and Gentiles. This enmity, however, is
done away with in Christ (Eph. 2:14–15).

The veil over their hearts would be destroyed for multitudes of
believing Gentiles (Isa. 25:7), and a veil of unbelief would form over the
hearts of many Jews. Isaiah predicted this judicial blindness for Israel
because they "despised and rejected" their Messiah:

Make the heart of this people [Israel] *fat, and make their ears heavy, and
shut their eyes; lest they see with their eyes, and hear with their ears, and
understand with their heart, and be converted, and be healed* (Isa. 6:10).

*It is a light thing that thou shouldest be my servant to raise up the tribes
of Jacob, and to restore the preserved of Israel; I will also give thee for a
light to the nations, that thou mayest be my salvation unto the end of the
earth* (Isa. 49:6).

Nearly twenty centuries of history attest to the truth of these words.
When Israel crucified and rejected their Messiah, a veil of unbelief set-
tled over the nation, and although some (a remnant) believe in the Lord
Jesus and are saved, blindness is still over the hearts and minds of most
Israelis (2 Cor. 3:14–15).

When the Jewish people rejected their Messiah, the gospel was taken
to the Gentiles (see Acts 28:28) and is now preached to the whole world,
Jewish and Gentile alike. That Gentiles should trust in a Jew for salvation is most unlikely, but true. That the very nation He came to bless
turned from Him seems most unlikely, but it is also true (Jn. 1:11–12).
That the Gentiles, who were not the people of God, should become the
people of God through faith in the Jewish Messiah seems preposterous,
but that is the plan God used to solve this prophetic paradox.

The Messiah Was to Have a Double Anointing— A Ministry of Mercy as Savior and a Ministry of Judgment as the Coming King

Since Christ, at His first advent, came to suffer for the sins of the people, we now know (although the Jews of Jesus' day found it hard to

realize) that His role as Judge and King will be fulfilled at His second advent. Concerning this subject, W. G. Moorehead wrote:

Isaiah, who describes with eloquence worthy of a prophet the glories of the Messiah's coming kingdom, also characterizes with the accuracy of the historian the humiliation, the trials, the agony which were to precede the triumph of the Redeemer of the world, presenting on the one hand a glorious King, Himself deity, "God with us," who has all power; yet, on the other hand, One whose visage was more marred than any man, His bones out of joint and dying of thirst (Ps. 22). How can He be both the great Davidic Monarch, restoring again the glory of Solomon's house, and also be a sacrifice bearing the sins of the people? Clearly, destinies so strongly contrasted could not be accomplished simultaneously. There is only one possible answer;. . . in the divine purpose the mighty drama is to be in two acts (His first advent and His second advent).

The *suffering Messiah* and His ministry of mercy are often presented in the same Scripture passage with His work as Judge and King. In Isaiah 61:1–2, the last phrase only describes His work of judgment at His second advent. The preceding part of the passage applies to His first advent:

The Spirit of the Lord GOD is upon me, because the LORD hath anointed me to preach good tidings unto the meek; he hath sent me to bind up the brokenhearted, to proclaim liberty to the captives, and the opening of the prison to those who are bound; To proclaim the acceptable year of the LORD, and the day of vengeance of our God; to comfort all that mourn.

This same intermingling of prophecy describing the Messiah's work at both advents—*to save* and *to judge*, His humiliation and work as the Redeemer at His first advent, and His work to establish His righteous kingdom at His second advent—is seen in many other Scriptures (i.e., Zech. 9:9–10; Mic. 5:1–4; Dan. 9:24; etc.). In studying messianic prophecy, it is important to determine if the first or second advent or both advents are in view.

When Christ, while speaking in the synagogue in Nazareth, applied the words of the Prophet Isaiah (61:1–2) to Himself (Lk. 4:17–21), He stopped His reading with the words, "To preach the acceptable year of the Lord" (v. 19). Why? He will not proclaim the day of vengeance of our God until His second advent.

The ancient rabbis, studying these and similar predictions about the coming Messiah, came to the conclusion that there must be *two Messiahs*, one a suffering Messiah and the other a conquering, judging

Messiah. They failed to see the great truth that there is only *one Messiah*, the Lord Jesus, who has two distinct tasks to perform, one at His first advent, "to make reconciliation for iniquity"; and the second when He returns to earth at His second advent as the mighty King "to bring in everlasting righteousness" (Dan. 9:24).

In Christ, the scores of apparently contradictory messianic prophecies referring either to His first advent or to His second advent, with their different objectives, are fully harmonized. These two advents of Christ are in contrast in such passages as Psalm 22 and Psalm 72; Psalm 69 and Psalm 89; Isaiah 53 and Isaiah 11. This same truth is fully revealed in the New Testament in such passages as 1 Peter 1:11, which speaks of "the sufferings of Christ" at His first advent and "the glory that should follow" at His second advent. Contrast also John 3:16–17 with Revelation 19:11–21; Luke 9:56 with Jude 14–15; and Luke 19:10 with 2 Thessalonians 1:7–10.

The Messiah Will be a Priest Upon His Throne

Thus speaketh the LORD of hosts: saying, Behold, the man whose name is THE BRANCH . . . he shall build the temple of the LORD . . . and shall sit and rule upon his throne; and he shall be a priest upon his throne (Zech. 6:12–13).

In Psalm 110:4, the Messiah is called "a priest forever after the order of Melchizedek." In Jeremiah 23:5, the Messiah is called "a righteous Branch, and a King." In the history of Israel, the chosen line of kings always came from the tribe of Judah (except among the ten tribes which split off to form the northern kingdom after the death of Solomon). Priests came from the tribe of Levi. Since Christ was from the tribe of Judah (Heb. 7:14), how could He also be a priest, since He could not come from two tribes (Judah and Levi)?

God solved this enigma as well. Christ is a King from the tribe of Judah; He will sit upon His throne on earth at His second advent. Christ also is a Priest whose priesthood is *patterned after the Aaronic priesthood* in which the priests offered sacrifices for the sins of the people; thus, Christ offered Himself as the once-for-all sacrifice for sin (Heb. 9:26). But, He was *made* a priest after the *order of Melchizedek* (Heb. 5:6; Ps. 110:4), who was both a king and a priest (Heb. 7:1–2). This intriguing subject of Christ's priesthood is fully explained in Hebrews chapters 7, 8 and 9. Again, the mystery was solved in Christ!

The Messiah, the Chosen Servant of the Lord, Would be Lovely, Most Pleasing to God, Yet He Would be Abhorred by the Nation of Israel

Isaiah 40:5 says that in the Messiah, the "glory of the LORD shall be revealed, and all flesh shall see it together." Then, in complete contrast, the Messiah is spoken of as the One who would be "despised and rejected of men," the One in whom the nation will see "no beauty" that they "should desire him" (Isa. 53:1–3).

In the history of Jesus, this paradox is explained. The Father said of Jesus, "This is my beloved Son, in whom I am well pleased" (Mt. 17:5). On the other hand, the people rejected Him; and no prophecies, other than those telling of His rejection, ever had a sadder fulfillment. The pathos of the Messiah's rejection is told by Jesus himself: "O Jerusalem, Jerusalem, thou that killest the prophets, and stonest them who are sent unto thee, how often would I have gathered thy children together, even as a hen gathereth her chickens under her wings, and ye would not!" (Mt. 23:37).

Those who hated Him "without a cause" were "more than the hairs of [his] head" (Ps. 69:4; cp. Jn. 15:25). The New Testament record tells us, "He came unto his own, and his own received him not" (Jn. 1:11).

Thirty Pieces of Silver Were Either the Price of Christ or the Price of the Potter's Field

And I said unto them, If ye think good, give me my price; and if not, for-bear. So they weighed for my price thirty pieces of silver. And the LORD said unto me, Cast it unto the potter—a lordly price that I was prized at of them. And I took the thirty pieces of silver, and cast them to the pot-ter in the house of the LORD (Zech. 11:12–13).

These are strange words which would be difficult to understand or reconcile with any specific event in history, were it not for the fulfill-ment as given in the New Testament. There we read that Judas covenanted with the chief priests to betray Christ and deliver Him to them, "and they bargained with him for thirty pieces of silver" (Mt. 26:15). When the heinousness of his crime dawned on him:

Judas . . . brought again the thirty pieces of silver to the chief priests and elders . . . And he cast down the pieces of silver in the temple, and depart-ed, and went and hanged himself. And the chief priests took the silver pieces, and said, It is not lawful to put them into the treasury, because it is the price of blood. And they took counsel, and bought with them the potter's field, to bury strangers in . . . Then was fulfilled that which was spoken by Jeremiah, the prophet, saying, And they took the thirty pieces of silver, the price of him that was valued . . . And gave them for the potter's field (Mt. 27:3, 5–7, 9–10).

Along with Judas, the nation of Israel sold Jesus and woefully underestimated Him. They sold Him for thirty pieces of silver, the price of a dead slave (Ex. 21:31). In so doing, the Jewish leaders expressed their hatred for and contempt of Him.

"No one can suppose that the perfect agreement of the Old Testament prediction with its New Testament fulfillment, centering about the exact amount of the sum of money (30 pieces of silver) could be accidental. Still less can it be conceived that the appropriation of the money to the purchase of the potter's field could have taken place without an overruling design" (*Book of Prophecy*, pp. 343–344).

In the fulfillment, all obscurity is removed, and the perfect harmony of the fulfillment with the prophecy is seen. "It was so exactly fulfilled that every one can see that the same God who spoke through the prophet had, by the secret operation of His omnipotent power, which extends even to the ungodly, so arranged matters that when Judas threw back their money and the chief priests purchased the potter's field, they [not only fulfilled prophecy, but] perpetuated the memorial of their sin against their Messiah, and called forth the vengeance of God against their nation" (David Baron, *Visions and Prophecies of Zechariah*, p. 409).

Prophecy Presents the Messiah as Rejected by Men and Forsaken by God and Describes Horrible Sufferings and Death for the One Who Perfectly Obeyed God at All Times

In Psalm 22:1, the Messiah prophetically cried out, "My God, my God, why hast thou forsaken me?" This desolate cry of the One forsaken by God and man is repeated in the New Testament, as Jesus was hanging on the cross: "And about the ninth hour Jesus cried with a loud voice, saying . . . My God, my God, why hast thou forsaken me?" (Mt. 27:46).

This forsaking of the righteous One in whom God delighted (Ps. 22:8) is all the more strange in that, from the beginning of human history, the fathers trusted in God and were delivered (Ps. 22:4–5); but not so in this instance. The strange enigma can only be fully understood through the explanation of the New Testament that in the sufferings and death of Jesus on the cross, God turned away from Him, for, "God made him [Christ], who knew no sin, to be sin for us, that we might be made the righteousness of God in him" (2 Cor. 5:21).

The Messiah was Wounded and Pierced, Yet Not a Bone was Broken

The Messiah was to be wounded in the house of His friends (Zech. 13:6) and have His hands and feet pierced (Ps. 22:16); yet, in some miraculous way, not one bone of the suffering Messiah was to be broken. In the Psalms, Jehovah said of the Messiah, "He keepeth all his bones; not one of them is broken" (Ps. 34:20; cp. Ex. 12:46).

At the crucifixion, when the Jews feared that the three men being crucified might linger on until death came too late to remove their bodies from the crosses before the beginning of the Sabbath, they sought permission from Pilate to break their legs, an act to hasten death so that they might be removed from the crosses sooner:

Then came the soldiers, and broke the legs of the first, and of the other who was crucified with him. But when they came to Jesus, and saw that he was dead already, they broke not his legs; But one of the soldiers, with a spear, pierced his side, and immediately came there out blood and water. And he that saw it bore witness, and his witness is true; and he knoweth that he saith true, that ye might believe. For these things were done, that the scripture should be fulfilled, A bone of him shall not be broken. And, again, another scripture saith, They shall look on him whom they pierced (Jn. 19:32–37).

What a marvelous miracle of divine providence: They broke the legs of the two who were crucified with Him, but *not* of Jesus; for prophecy had said, "A bone of him shall not be broken." They pierced His hands, His feet and His side, and each time the weapons struck *between* the bones and did not break them.

The Messiah Was to be Cut Off and Pour Out His Soul Unto Death, Yet God Would Prolong His Days and Divide Him a Portion With the Great

The glorious facts of the Messiah's atoning death and resurrection are prophetically stated in language which is at first obscure but which becomes clear when fulfilled in one of the most thrilling prophetic paradoxes in the entire realm of Scripture.

In the New Testament we read:

He [Jesus] *humbled himself and became obedient unto death, even the death of the cross. Wherefore, God also hath highly exalted him, and given him a name which is above every name, That at the name of Jesus every knee should bow . . . And that every tongue should confess that Jesus Christ is Lord, to the glory of God, the Father* (Phil. 2:8–11).

Mankind despised Jesus and set Him at nought (Isa. 53:3); but in His time, God made Him "higher than the kings of the earth" (Ps. 89:27). The Old Testament prophets and their readers puzzled over this mystery, but everything was made plain when, in the New Testament, Jesus the Christ died for our sins and was raised from the dead on the third day.

Prophecies Concerning
the Suffering, Death
and Resurrection of the Messiah
(An Examination of Psalm 22 and Isaiah 53)

Psalm 22

The miracle of the 22nd Psalm is this: Crucifixion was a Roman and Grecian custom unknown to the Jews until the days of their captivity (600 B.C.). The Jews executed their criminals by stoning; and yet, written 1,000 years before the time of Christ by a man who had never seen or heard of such a method of execution, Psalm 22 gives a graphic portrayal of death by crucifixion!

The messianic nature of this Psalm is almost universally admitted by devout students. D. M. Pantone wrote:

Psalm 22, one of David's Psalms, reveals someone—Messiah—dying an awful death, under very peculiar circumstances. The ancient document says, "the assembly of the wicked have enclosed me; they pierced my hands and my feet. I may count all my bones; they look and stare upon me" (v. 16–17). Crucifixion in David's time was unknown among the Jews; yet the piercing of hands and feet together with the partial stripping—"counting all the bones"—obviously means crucifixion: the crucified are pierced only in their hands and feet, and stripped for exposure. Would a false Messiah have chosen this passage for fulfillment?

This old document (Ps. 22) holds the very crucifixion cry, for the Psalm opens with it—"My God, my God, why hast thou forsaken me?" (v. 1). Not a jot or tittle of this Psalm has miscarried: exactly as in His birth and in His ministry, so also in His death—but more so—the ancient document is a photograph of the fact, fulfilled in flawless detail" (*Dawn Magazine*).

The Forsaken One

Christ on the cross identified Himself with the One spoken of in this Psalm by quoting its first verse: "My God, my God, why hast thou forsaken me?" (Mt. 27:46). This Psalm has been called "The Psalm of Sobs" (Bishop Alexander, *Witness of the Psalms to Christ*).

The Hebrew shows not one completed sentence in the opening verses, but a series of brief ejaculations, like the gasps of a dying man whose breath and strength are failing, and who can only utter a word or two at a time: "My God—My God—why forsaken me—far from helping me—words of my roaring" presenting a picture overwhelmingly pathetic: the suffering Savior, forsaken by God, gasping for life, unable to articulate one continuous sentence . . . The writer thus forecasts the mystery of the cross which remained unsolved for a thousand years. It was like a dark cavern at the time but when the gospel narrative portrays Jesus as the crucified One, it is like putting a lighted torch in the cavern (A. T. Pierson, *Living Oracles*, p. 107).

Periods of Light and Darkness

In verse 2 one sees alternate periods of light and darkness: "O my God, I cry in the daytime, but thou hearest not; and in the night season, and am not silent" (Ps. 22:2).

In the New Testament account of the crucifixion of Christ, we read, "Now from the sixth hour there was darkness over all the land unto the ninth hour" (Mt. 27:45).

Righteous, Yet Forsaken by God

In verses 3–5 we see a prophetic discussion of this strange anomaly: a truly righteous One forsaken by God. It had never happened before in the history of the "fathers." They trusted and were delivered; the

Messiah on the cross was forsaken. Christ on the cross was forsaken by God and man.

They Mocked Him

Verses 6–8 tell of those who reproached and mocked Him: "All they who see me laugh me to scorn; they shoot out the lip, they shake the head, saying, He trusted on the LORD that he would deliver him; let him deliver him, seeing he delighted in him" (vv. 7–8).

The New Testament relates how the people ridiculed and derided Christ on the cross, using almost the identical words which the prophet used: "Likewise also the chief priests, mocking Him . . . said . . . He trusted in God; let him deliver him now (Mt. 27:41, 43).

His Weakness, Thirst and Exposure to Public Scorn

In the prophetic record, further startling details are given: "They gaped upon me . . . I am poured out like water, and all my bones are out of joint: my heart is like wax; it is melted within me. My strength is dried up like a potsherd, and my tongue cleaveth to my jaws; and thou hast brought me into the dust of death" (vv. 13–15).

The Messiah's exposure to public scorn—"they gaped upon me" (v. 13)—was fulfilled in the New Testament when, at the cross, the people "sitting down . . . watched him" (Mt. 27:36). His extreme weakness, perspiration and thirst under the pitiless beating of the oriental sun were predicted: "I am poured out like water . . . my strength is dried up like a potsherd, and my tongue cleaveth to my jaws" (vv. 14–15).

The forsaken sufferer in the New Testament expressed in one simple statement His weakness and thirst: "After this Jesus, knowing that all things were now accomplished, that the scripture might be fulfilled, saith, I thirst (Jn. 19:28).

He Died of a Broken Heart

One weeps in heart thinking of the Messiah's horrible sufferings, the agony from dislocated bones caused by the weight of the body suspended only by the nails in the hands and feet, "all my bones are out of joint" (v. 14). Add to that the mental and spiritual torture so great that it literally broke His heart: "my heart is like wax; it is melted within me" (v. 14). At last His sufferings were ended by death, "thou hast brought me into the dust of death" (v. 15).

There is evidence from the New Testament record that Jesus died of a broken heart. When the Roman soldier "pierced his side . . . immediately came there out blood and water" indicating that the heart had been ruptured before it was pierced by the spear, probably from the great emotional strain Christ had suffered. The lymphatic fluid apparently had separated from the red blood, producing "blood and water." The word "lymph" comes from the Latin *lympha*, meaning *water* (cp. 1 Jn. 5:6).

The Parting of His Garments

For exquisite detail dramatically fulfilled, verse 18 is the gem of all prophecy: "They part my garments among them, and cast lots upon my vesture." The divinely inspired prophet, looking down through ten centuries of time, saw and recorded an incident connected with the crucifixion which seems so trivial and unimportant that one wonders why it is referred to at all—unless it was to inform us that the omniscient God wrote the prophecy and the omnipotent God brought it to fulfillment.

In the New Testament account of the crucifixion of Christ, when they pierced His hands and feet, that additional, *unimportant* detail about the disposition of the Messiah's garments was mentioned. Roman soldiers, ignorant of both God and prophecy and knowing nothing of the sacred importance of what they were doing, fulfilled to the letter that age-old prediction:

> Then the soldiers, when they had crucified Jesus, took his garments, and made four parts, to every soldier a part; and also his coat. Now the coat was without seam, woven from the top throughout. They said, therefore, among themselves, Let us not tear it, but cast lots for it, whose it shall be; that the scripture might be fulfilled, which saith, They parted my raiment among them, and for my vesture they did cast lots. These things, therefore, the soldiers did (Jn. 19:23–24).

And so, an obscure prophecy, hidden in the Old Testament for a thousand years, sprang forth as a witness, a living miracle, proving again that God spoke in the Old Testament and *fulfilled* in the New Testament. This prophecy shows that the predictions concerning the Messiah in the Old Testament were fulfilled in the Christ of the Gospels, thereby giving a satisfying demonstration of the divine origin of both Testaments.

The Resurrection of the Messiah

The Messiah, so cruelly put to death, would be helped (v. 19), delivered (v. 20) and saved from the lion's mouth (v. 21). His prayer would be answered (v. 21, "thou hast heard me"). Verse 21 is the end of a section. Verse 22 begins a new section, and the Messiah, now gloriously delivered and resurrected, says: "I will declare thy name unto my brethren; in the midst of the congregation will I praise thee."

The New Testament abounds with evidence that although Christ died and was forsaken by God and man, still God raised Him from the dead on the third day: "ye have taken [Christ], and by wicked hands have crucified and slain; Whom God hath raised up, having loosed the pains of death, because it was not possible that he should be held by it" (Acts 2:23–24).

"The predictions concerning Christ in this chapter," wrote Moses Margoliouth, "are so numerous and so minute that they could not possibly have been dictated by any but by Him to whom all things are naked and open, and who worketh all things according to the counsel of His own will. The most *insignificant* circumstances connected with our Lord's death are set forth with as much accuracy as those which are *most important* . . . What could be more unlikely than that Messiah should be crucified when crucifixion was not a Jewish but a Roman punishment? And yet David in this Psalm predicted such would be the case centuries before Rome was founded" and ten centuries before the prophecy was fulfilled!

Isaiah 53

This remarkable prophecy of the sufferings and exaltation of the Messiah was written 700 years before the time of Christ. It reads more like "an historical summary of the Gospel narrative of the sufferings of Christ and the glory that should follow, instead of a prophecy" (David Baron). With this agrees Augustine, who said, "Me thinks Isaiah writes not a prophecy but a Gospel." And another commentator said, "It reads as if it had been written beneath the cross of Golgotha. It is the deepest and the loftiest thing that Old Testament prophecy, outstripping itself, has ever achieved." A. T. Pierson wrote:

This chapter is a bundle of paradoxes, or apparent contradictions, as numerous as the verses in the chapter. In fact, it was *designed* to present a prophetic enigma which only the person (and work) of the Christ of the New Testament can solve. He is a root out of the dry ground—yet fruitful; He has no form nor beauty—yet He is the chosen Servant of God; He is despised and rejected of men— yet He is the appointed Savior; He suffers unto death—yet He survives; He has no offspring—yet He has a numerous seed; men would make His grave with the wicked—yet He is buried with the rich; He suffers unbelievable adversity—yet He enjoys prosperity; He is triumphed over—yet He triumphs; He is condemned—yet He justifies the condemned. These paradoxes remained a problem until the cross was set up, the sepulcher burst open, and the Son of God who came to die went up to reign (*Living Oracles*, p. 110).

The Suffering Messiah, Jehovah's Servant

Unfortunately, the chapter division comes at the wrong place. It should begin with Isaiah 52:13, which opens with the words, "Behold, my servant," and that is the subject of this entire section (Isa. 52:13—53:12).

The first question to be answered is, "of whom speaketh the prophet this? Of himself, or of some other man?" (Acts. 8:34). The only possible correct answer is, this prophecy speaks of an individual, the Messiah, and there is only one person in the history of the world who fulfills the prophecy, Jesus Christ of the New Testament. Professor James Orr observed:

Let anyone steep his mind in the contents of this chapter and then read what is said about Jesus in the Gospels, and as he stands underneath the cross, see if there is not the most perfect correspondence between the two. In Jesus of Nazareth alone in all history, but in Him perfectly, has this prophecy found fulfillment.

Some unbelievers have sought to interpret this passage as referring to "suffering Israel," the nation, rather than to the suffering Messiah. But the following five facts prove the theme of Isaiah 53 to be the Messiah, not the Jewish people.

First, this entire prophecy speaks of an *individual*. It is "*he* shall grow up" (v. 2); "*he* is despised . . . a *man* of sorrows" (v. 3); "*he* was wounded" (v. 5); and so forth throughout the chapter.

Second, verse 8 is conclusive: the sufferer was stricken for the transgressions of "my people" (Israel). He is an individual who suffers vicariously *for* the people; therefore, He cannot *be* the people.

Third, He is an *innocent* sufferer (vv. 7, 9), which could never be said of the nation of Israel.

Fourth, He is a *voluntary* sufferer who willingly "poured out his soul unto death" (v. 12), again depicting the death of an individual, not a nation.

Fifth, He is an *unresisting* sufferer who "opened not his mouth" (v. 7), which could never be said of the nation of Israel.

The meaning could not be more clear: Isaiah 53 describes an *innocent, voluntary, unresisting individual who suffered vicariously for God's people, Israel*. When Jesus of Nazareth came 700 years later and died on the cross, *these predictions were fulfilled with a literalness that astonishes and an exactness that parallels mathematical certainty.*

The Messiah's Astonishing Exaltation (52:13)

Behold, my servant shall deal prudently; he shall be exalted and extolled, and be very high.

Before the depth of the Messiah's humiliation is presented, we are at the outset assured of His final *victory* and *glory*. Franz Delitzsch called attention to the progressive nature of the words "exalted," "extolled" and "raised." He said: "From these words we obtain this chain of thought: He will rise up, He will raise Himself still higher, He will stand on high." And Stier rightly connected this with the three principal steps in the fulfillment of the prediction in Jesus after His death, namely His *resurrection*, His *ascension* and His sitting down in *exaltation* at the *right hand of God.*

Here, then, we are at once confronted with the Messiah's final end. To prepare us, as it were, for the shock of His temporary abasement, the "Servant of the Lord (after His sufferings) is seen rising from stage to stage; and at last He reaches an immeasurable height that towers above everything beside" (Delitzsch, *The Servant of the Lord*, p. 58).

The New Testament is very clear concerning the final exaltation of Christ after His sufferings and death:

Who, being the brightness of his glory, and the express image of his person, and upholding all things by the word of his power, when he had by himself purged our sins [by His atoning death on the cross], *sat down on the right hand of the Majesty on high* (Heb. 1:3).

Christ Jesus . . . being in the form of God, thought it not robbery to be equal with God . . . humbled himself and became obedient unto death, even the death of the cross. Wherefore, God also hath highly exalted him, and given him a name which is above every name (Phil. 2:5–6, 8–9).

The Messiah's Shocking Abuse (Isa. 52:14)

As many were astounded at thee—his visage was so marred more than any man, and his form more than the sons of men.

If the Messiah's exaltation (v. 13) is astonishingly high, His sufferings are even more astonishing: "Just as many were astonished at him, for so disfigured was he that his appearance was not human, and his form was not like that of the children of men" (trans. by Delitzsch).

During the terrible hours before His crucifixion, the Lord Jesus was brutally manhandled, buffeted, scourged and abused in other ways.

The scourging itself was violent, inhuman. The scourge was usually made of leather thongs fastened to a handle. At the ends of the thongs were often fastened bits of sharpened metal or rock which cut and lacerated the flesh of the victim and turned the back into a bleeding pulp.

On the cross, the crown of thorns, the nails driven through His quivering flesh and the consequent agony of crucifixion, in which every nerve and muscle became a flame of torture, added to the excruciating mental agony and soul suffering. Jesus' features became so marred and distorted that He no longer resembled a man. This horrifying fact is clearly revealed in the Old Testament and just as clearly documented in the New Testament: "Then Pilate, therefore, took Jesus, and scourged him. And the soldiers plaited a crown of thorns, and put it on his head" (Jn. 19:1–2).

There are thorns in Bible lands having spines two to three inches long. When dried, they are very hard, pointed and sharp as needles. Such a *crown*, if pressed down on the brow, would puncture the skin in many places and cause pain and a flow of blood which resulted in matted, disheveled hair, presenting a horrible appearance:

Then they spat in his face, and buffeted him; and other smote him with the palms of their hands . . . And they stripped him, and put on him a scarlet robe. And when they had plaited a crown of thorns, they put it upon his head, and a reed in his right hand . . . And they spat upon him, and took the reed, and smote him on the head (Mt. 26:67; 27:28–30).

God permitted and Jesus endured this horrible suffering, not only to fulfill the prophetic picture, but to suffer in our stead. Who, but the true Messiah, would want to be a Messiah like that?

In the hours before being nailed to the cross, Jesus' *face* was marred, and on the cross, His *form* was marred, thereby completely fulfilling the prediction by Isaiah. The bloody sweat, the traces of the crown of thorns, the spittle on His face and the smiting on the head all contributed to the disfigurement of His face. The scourging, the buffeting, the nails driven through His hands and feet, the weight of the body pulling it out of joint and the spear thrust through His side distorted His body. Add to all that the extreme mental anguish and grief of soul, and the result was one so marred that He no longer resembled a man. How much He loved us; how much He paid for our redemption!

As we humbly contemplate the intensity of the dreadful sufferings of the Savior, may our hearts be "bowed with shame and sorrow for the sin which was the cause of it all, and may we have a greater love and undying gratitude to Him who bore all this for us" (David Baron).

The Messiah Will Bring a Message that Will Startle Many Nations (Isa. 52:15)

So shall he sprinkle many nations; the kings shall shut their mouths at him; for that which had not been told them shall they not see, and that which they had not heard shall they consider.

God himself, in the person of His Son, suffered so violently, creating so ghastly a scene, that it has impressed all ages. The memory of Calvary startles the most dormant, pricks the most calloused, stirs the most lethargic. Men now understand both the love of God and the wisdom of God; Calvary reveals them. Men see both the grace of God and how God can bestow righteousness on sinners who believe, "For he hath made him, who knew no sin, to be sin for us, that we might be made the righteousness of God in him" (2 Cor. 5:21). The gospel will startle many into believing.

The Messiah Brings a Message that Will be Disbelieved by Israel (Isa. 53:1)

Who hath believed our report? And to whom is the arm of the LORD revealed?

Although the shocking message of a suffering Messiah startled many nations, it found few believers among the Messiah's own brethen, the Jewish people.

In the New Testament we find the fulfillment of this prediction:

But though he had done so many miracles before them, yet they believed not on him; That the saying of Isaiah, the prophet, might be fulfilled, which he spoke, Lord, who hath believed our report? And to whom hath the arm of the Lord been revealed? (Jn. 12:37–38).

The Messiah's Supernatural Birth and Spiritual Growth (Isa. 53:2a)

For he shall grow up before him like a tender plant, and like a root out of a dry ground.

The Messiah's supernatural birth is intimated in the phrase, "As a root out of a dry ground." A root growing out of dry ground is a miracle because one essential element, moisture, is missing. The Messiah's birth was to be a miracle—the miracle of the virgin birth.

Notice also another paradox. His supernatural yet natural growth. He will grow up (normally, much as other children), and yet it will be "before him." That is, the Messiah shall grow up in Jehovah's presence and under His watch care. Here too He will owe nothing to natural surroundings, for the Messiah shall be "a tender plant . . . out of a dry ground." That is, the Messiah will be a precious, wholesome plant in His youth, growing up before the Heavenly Father's watchful care, yet He will grow up in the midst of the universal spiritual dearth of the nation, in a desert of hardness, sin and unbelief. But it will be a normal process; He will "grow up." He will not "burst upon the world all at once, in a sudden splendour of daring and achievement: He will conform to God's slow, silent law of growth" (James Culross).

It is amazing that God foretold the manner of His coming to earth, the growth of His childhood and the spiritually of His childhood. And, when the Messiah came, everything was fulfilled exactly as had been predicted. The Messiah did not come as a full-grown King in His might, with dash and splendor; that is reserved for His second advent. In the New Testament, we read of the child Jesus, "And the child grew, and became strong in spirit, filled with wisdom; and the grace of God was upon him" (Lk. 2:40).

The Messiah's Generation Would Fail to See and Appreciate His Greatness (Isa. 53:2b)

He hath no form nor comeliness, and when we shall see him, there is no beauty that we should desire him.

When the Messiah came, the people were looking for a mighty king and a political reformer and were, therefore, disappointed with Him. Men did not see His beauty—the beauty of holiness—nor did they understand His mission. He did not answer to the worldly ideal. Having misread the prophecies, they found nothing to charm or attract them in Jehovah's servant when He came. The work of the Messiah in His first advent—to make His soul an "offering for sin"—was foreign to their ideas of what the Messiah should be.

The Messiah Would be Despised and Rejected of Men (Isa. 53:3–4)

He is despised and rejected of men, a man of sorrows, and acquainted with grief, and we hid as it were our faces from him; he was despised, and we esteemed him not . . . we did esteem him stricken, smitten of God and afflicted.

"Rejected of men," says David Baron, "means actually 'rejected by men of high rank.'" That is, He would have no men of high standing, no *important* men, few men of distinction to support Him and His program with their authority and influence.

This proved to be true in the life of Jesus, as the New Testament record reveals: "Then answered them the Pharisees, Are ye also deceived? Have any of the rulers or of the Pharisees believed on him?" (Jn. 7:47–48; see context).

Who but the infinite God, who knows the end from the beginning, would dare frame a prophecy like that, presenting the Messiah as being without the support of the leaders of the people? But history fully confirmed the accuracy of the prediction.

The Messiah Would be Known as a Man of Sorrows, Smitten of God, Afflicted (Isa. 53:3–4)

He is . . . a man of sorrows, and acquainted with grief, and we hid as it were our faces from him . . . we did esteem him stricken, smitten of God, and afflicted.

The point being emphasized is that the Messiah would be "a man of pains" (Heb.). He would experience sorrow of heart in all its forms.

Jesus' sorrow came not only as He compassionately suffered with the ills of humanity—a sympathetic suffering—but also when He was repelled in His efforts to bless. His sorrow was overwhelming when the people rejected Him and continued in their lost condition. His sorrows were multiplied when men of high rank and position turned from Him. Instead of considering Him precious, they "esteemed him not"—"estimated Him as nothing" (Martin Luther).

Worst of all, the people to whom He came considered Him "smitten of God": "He came unto his own, and his own received him not" (Jn. 1:11). They did not realize that He suffered to redeem them and that He permitted Himself to be "made a curse" that He might save those for whom He suffered: "Christ hath redeemed us from the curse of the law, being made a curse for us; for it is written, Cursed is everyone that hangeth on a tree" (Gal. 3:13).

The Messiah's Vicarious Sufferings (Isa. 53:4–6, 8, 10–12)

Surely he hath borne our griefs, and carried our sorrows . . . he was wounded for our transgressions, he was bruised for our iniquities; the chastisement for our peace was upon him, and with his stripes we are healed . . . the LORD *hath laid on him the iniquity of us all . . . for the transgression of my people was he stricken . . . thou shalt make his soul an offering for sin . . . he shall bear their iniquities . . . he bore the sin of many.*

"The Divine Author makes it impossible for any ingenuity or learning to eliminate the doctrine of vicarious atonement from this passage by presenting it so often, and in forms so varied and still the same, that he who succeeds in expelling it in one place is compelled to meet it in another" (Dr. Alexander).

The outstanding element of this chapter is the *vicarious, substitutionary sufferings of the Messiah.* "Marvelous chapter," comments A. T. Pierson, "containing only twelve verses, yet fourteen times announcing the doctrine of the vicarious sacrifice for all human sin." The whole section (Isa. 52:13—53:12) overflows with this concept, and the mystery was never solved until the Lord Jesus was "made . . . sin for us" (2 Cor. 5:21) and "died for our sins" (1 Cor. 15:3).

Jehovah "hath caused to meet with overwhelming force in Him the iniquity of us all" (Heb.). The Messiah was the divine Redeemer on whom fell "all the fiery rays of judgment which would have fallen on mankind" (Baron). How wonderful is God's grace through Christ's substitutionary atonement! The cross became Christ's deepest humiliation and His highest glory—the appointed means of bringing salvation to men.

When the Lord Jesus came, He fulfilled these messianic predictions by His atoning death on the cross: "Who his own self bore our sins in his own body on the tree, that we, being dead to sins, should live unto righteousness; by whose stripes ye were healed" (1 Pet. 2:24).

The Messiah Would Suffer Willingly and Without Complaint (Isa. 53:7)

He was oppressed, and he was afflicted, yet he opened not his mouth; he is brought as a lamb to the slaughter, and as a sheep before her shearers is dumb, so he openeth not his mouth.

Other sufferers usually register murmuring or complaining, especially when they are unjustly treated; but not so with the suffering Messiah. He voluntarily submitted Himself to His appointed task of bearing our sins and went as a lamb to the slaughter. "In sublime and magnanimous silence Messiah will endure to the uttermost, because Jehovah wills it . . . And here we look down into the unfathomed mystery of infinite love" (Culross).

In the New Testament, when Jesus was beaten, falsely accused, mistreated, mocked, spat upon, persecuted, manhandled, scourged and crucified, there were no flames of resentment, no incriminations against His executioners, no loud complaints, but, rather, a prayer for His persecutors.

After many false witnesses appeared against Him, Jesus "held his peace"; and the high priest, wondering about His silence, asked "Answerest thou nothing?" (see Mt. 26:59–63). Jesus' prayer, while suffering the tortures of crucifixion, was, "Father, forgive them; for they know not what they do" (Lk. 23:34).

This entire scene was so unusual, so contrary to nature and human experience, that one cannot help but be struck by both the strange prophecy and its even more remarkable fulfillment.

The Messiah Would Have No Advocate to Plead His Cause, No Friend to Declare His Innocence (Isa. 53:8)

He was taken from prison and from judgment; and who shall declare his generation?

An alternate reading of the last phrase is, "And who [among] his generation shall declare [his innocence]?" "The Sanhedrin had the custom in 'trials for life' to call on those who knew anything in favor of the accused to come forward and declare it" (David Baron in *The Servant of Jehovah,* p. 106). This was not observed in the trial of Jesus; but, rather, the proceedings at His hasty, mock, illegal trial before the Sanhedrin were in flagrant contradiction to their own regulations and against all standards of right and fairness.

Jesus had to appear alone and undefended before the corrupt Jewish hierarchy and the representatives of the greatest Gentile power on earth at that time. *Not one person appeared to take His part.* Judas betrayed Him; Peter denied Him with oaths; and the other disciples "forsook him, and fled" (Mt. 26:56). Many of the women who had, during His ministry, ministered to Him, stood "beholding [from] afar off" when He was crucified (Mt. 27:55). In the hour of His greatest need, humanly speaking, *not one person stood by Him.* While it is true that after the weary hours of suffering had numbed His broken body, His mother Mary, a few faithful women and His beloved disciple John "stood by" at the cross; but during His trial and the early hours of His crucifixion, He was left alone—absolutely alone. Never in the history of the world has anyone been so completely forsaken by friends and loved ones as was Jesus.

Jesus was not arrested by proper officials but by a mob, the rabble, "a great multitude with swords and clubs, from the chief priests and elders of the people (Mt. 26:47). Even Jesus himself commented on the inconsistency of their approach: "Are ye come out as against a thief with swords and clubs to take me? I sat daily with you teaching in the temple, and ye laid no hold on me. But all this was done, that the scriptures of the prophets might be fulfilled" (Mt. 26:55–56).

"False witnesses" were suborned to testify against Him, "to put him to death" (Mt. 26:59). He was tried at night, which was illegal.

In the Roman court, when Pilate sought in vain for a cause to justly condemn Him, he asked the people, "what evil hath he done?" The only answer he received was the shouting of the mob, encouraged by their leaders, "Let him be crucified" (Mt. 27:23). When Pilate saw that words of reason and justice "could prevail nothing" and that a worse "tumult" was developing (Mt. 27:24), he weakly washed his hands of the affair and turned Jesus over to them that they might crucify Him (Mt. 27:26). This was the worst miscarriage of justice in the annals of history.

But Jesus' innocence, as attested to by Pilate—"I find no fault in him" (Jn. 19:4)—fulfilled the messianic prophecy of old, "he had done no violence, neither was any deceit in his mouth" (Isa. 53:9).

The Messiah's Humiliation Would End at the Moment of Death, and Although Men Planned His Burial With the Wicked, Providence Planned It With the Rich (Isa. 53:9).

And he made his grave with the wicked, and with the rich in his death because he had done no violence, neither was any deceit in his mouth.

Franz Delitzsch translates this passage as follows: "They [men] appointed him his grave with the wicked [but] he was a rich man after his death."

"Dying as a criminal, ordinarily His body would have been flung over the wall to be burned like offal in the fires of Topheth (west of Jerusalem); but when His vicarious sufferings were finished, no further indignity was permitted to His lifeless body" (A. T. Pierson). "And this remarkable coincidence," wrote Franz Delitizsch, "is truly wonderful if we reflect that the Jewish rulers would have given to Jesus the same dishonorable burial as that given to the two thieves, but the Roman authorities handed over His body to Joseph the Arimathean, a 'rich man' (Mt. 27:57) who placed it in his sepulcher in his own garden. And at once we see an agreement between the gospel history and the prophetic words which could only be the work of the God of both prophecy and its fulfillment, inasmuch as no suspicion could possibly arise of there having been any human design of bringing the former into conformity with the latter."

The reason given for His honorable burial, which was so different from what had been planned for Him by His enemies, was, "because he had done no violence, neither was any deceit in his mouth" (Isa. 53:9). This is another reiteration of the absolute *innocence* of the divine sufferer.

The New Testament account of Jesus' burial records this perfect fulfillment:

When the evening was come, there came a rich man of Arimathea, named Joseph, who also himself was Jesus' disciple; He went to Pilate, and begged the body of Jesus. Then Pilate commanded the body to be delivered. And when Joseph had taken the body, he wrapped it in a clean linen cloth, And laid it in his own new tomb, which he had hewn out in the rock (Mt. 27:57–60).

The Messiah Would Be Resurrected to See His Seed, the Fruits of His Travail (Isa. 53:10)

When thou shalt make his soul an offering for sin, he shall see his seed, he shall prolong his days, and the pleasure of the LORD shall prosper in his hand.

After the Messiah's offering of Himself as a trespass offering, God will "prolong his days" in resurrection, and He shall "see his seed"—saved souls—as the result of His sacrifice.

The fulfillment of this paradox, as we have already seen, is in the death and resurrection of Jesus who, "died for our sins according to the scriptures; And . . . rose again the third day according to the scriptures" (1 Cor. 15:3–4).

The Messiah's resurrection is in harmony with other Old Testament Scriptures, such as Psalm 16:10: "For thou wilt not leave my soul in sheol, neither wilt thou permit thine Holy One to see corruption."

Moreover, the will of God will "prosper" in the Messiah's hand. The Messiah will accomplish God's will with zeal, and He will indeed bring salvation and righteousness to Israel and the nations (see Isa. 42:4).

The New Testament tells of the glorious resurrection of Christ as well as the beginning of His ministry after His resurrection, working through His disciples, by which multitudes were and are being added to the Church. "About three thousand souls" were saved and added to the Church on one occasion (Acts 2:41); and "the number of the men was about five thousand" who were added on another occasion (Acts 4:4).

During the last nineteen centuries of Church history, untold millions have believed in Christ and been saved. He has indeed seen His seed, and the will of God is prospering in His hand. The gospel of Christ will eventually, after His second advent, come to final and complete triumph, and then "the earth shall be full of the knowledge of the LORD, as the waters cover the sea" (Isa. 11:9). Truly, the Captain of our salvation is "bringing many sons unto glory" (Heb. 2:10).

The Messiah Will Satisfy God with His Sacrifice and Through Knowing the Messiah Many Shall Be Justified (Isa. 53:11)

He shall see of the travail of his soul, and shall be satisfied; by his knowledge shall my righteous servant justify many; for he shall bear their iniquities.

This is a forecast of the tremendous truth, so fully developed by Paul in the New Testament, of *justification by faith*, salvation by grace—because Christ died for our sins and purchased a full redemption for all. This truth of justification by faith is the grand, central truth of the New Testament: "Even the righteousness of God which is by faith of Jesus Christ unto all and upon all them that believe . . . Being justified freely by his grace through the redemption that is in Christ Jesus" (Rom. 3:22, 24); "For by grace are ye saved through faith" (Eph. 2:8; cp. Rom. 4:5–6; 5:15–19; Ti. 3:5; etc.).

Lest we forget that all grace bestowed upon believers is based on the Messiah's sacrifice, we again are reminded that "He shall bear their iniquities," observes Dr. Alexander, further stating that there is an "antithesis here suggesting the idea of exchange or mutual substitution; *they* shall receive His righteousness, and *He* shall bear the heavy burden of their iniquities." This, of course, is compatible with the doctrine of the New Testament: "For he [God] hath made him [Christ], who knew no sin, to be sin for us, that we might be made the righteousness of God in him" (2 Cor. 5:21).

The Messiah's Death Will Involve Strange Circumstances (Isa. 53:12)

He was numbered with the transgressors; and he bore the sin of many, and made intercession for the transgressors.

Similar to the account of the disposition of the Messiah's garments in Psalm 22:18, here is a comparable incident showing true detail in prophecy which marks it as genuine.

In verse 12, the word "transgressors" does not refer to ordinary sinners but to criminals (Heb. *poshim*, meaning *criminals, open transgressors of the law of God and man*). Furthermore, Delitzsch, Hengstenberg, Baron and others translate the reflexive verb used here, "He permitted Himself, voluntarily, to be numbered or 'reckoned' with criminals," showing again the Messiah's willingness to suffer all that the Father had planned for Him.

It is of more than passing interest to recall that Christ himself quoted Isaiah 53:12 just before His own crucifixion: "This that is written must yet be accomplished in me, And he was reckoned among the transgressors" (Lk. 22:37).

And so, as Delitzsch observed, this prediction and its fulfillment become "one of those remarkable coincidences which was brought about by providence between the prophecies and our Savior's passion," that Christ should have been crucified between two thieves (lit., *robbers*) [see Lk. 23:39–43].

Much has already been said about the vicarious nature of the Messiah's sufferings as seen in Isaiah 53. In the closing verse, that fact again is stressed: "He himself bore the sin of many" (lit. trans.).

Those familiar with the New Testament will recall many Scriptures which set forth the substitutionary nature of the death of Christ, such as:

But now once, in the end of the ages, hath he [Christ] *appeared to put away sin by the sacrifice of himself . . . So Christ was once offered to bear the sins of many* (Heb. 9:26, 28).
For Christ also hath once suffered for sins, the just for the unjust, that he might bring us to God (1 Pet. 3:18).

Many volumes have been written showing the wonders of the messianic prophecies in Isaiah 53 and their fulfillment in the atoning death of Jesus as described in the New Testament. By carefully examining these parallel Old Testament and New Testament passages, the faith of many will either be generated or confirmed in both the supernatural character of the prophecies and their fulfillment. This clearly shows that Scripture has upon it the stamp of its divine Author, the mark of Heaven, the imprint of eternity.

Chapter Six

Prophecies Describing the Messianic Offices of Christ

Christ, the Anointed One

Both the words "Christ" (Greek) and "Messiah" (Hebrew) mean *Anointed One* (for examples of the use of "anointed" in the Old Testament, see Lev. 4:3, 5; 1 Sam. 2:10; Ps. 2:2; Dan. 9:25–26; etc.). The word "anointed" occurs most frequently in Leviticus, 1 and 2 Samuel and the Psalms. The term "Messiah" (*anointed*) is applied to the high priest (Lev. 4:3, 5, 16; 6:22), who was a type or picture of Christ our High Priest. It occurs 18 times in 1 and 2 Samuel, but not always with messianic connotation. It is found ten times in the Psalms, but again, not always with messianic import. Psalms 2:2; 20:6; 28:8; 84:9; 89:51; 132:10, 17 are, we believe, messianic. Psalm 2:2 and Daniel 9:25–26 are outstanding passages referring to the coming Messiah.

Since the fall of man and his consequent separation from God (Rom. 5:12), mankind has needed a Mediator, a Redeemer who can fill man's three basic needs.

First, sin left man in spiritual darkness, ignorant of God. Because of this, man needs knowledge of the Word, the will and the ways of God. Man needs a *prophet*. Second, sin left man guilty, lost, separated from God; hence, he needs forgiveness of sin, restoration of a righteous character and restoration to divine fellowship. For this, man needs a *priest*. Third, sin, which is rebellion against God's government, left man with a rebellious nature that expresses itself in antagonism to his fellowmen. Since man is a social creature, a unit in society, he needs authoritative governmental supervision; hence, he needs a *king*.

In the Old Testament economy, God provided these basic needs of mankind through His chosen prophets, priests and kings, but all human instruments come short and fail; therefore, God planned from the beginning that He would provide the perfect *Prophet, Priest* and *King* for mankind in the perfect One, His only begotten Son.

In Old Testament times, these three classes of public servants—prophets, priests and kings—were consecrated to their offices by an anointing with oil (prophets, see 1 Ki. 19:16; priests, see Ex. 29:21; Lev. 8:12; kings, see 1 Sam. 10:1; 16:12–13).

Christ as Prophet

The Old Testament prophet represented God to the nation; he gave His words and message to the people. When the Messiah came, He was to represent God perfectly and completely in person, as well as in words, to Israel and to the world. When Jesus came, He proved to be God's perfect Prophet:

No man hath seen God at any time; the only begotten Son, who is in the bosom of the Father, he hath declared [revealed, manifested] *him* (Jn. 1:18).
Jesus saith unto him . . . He that hath seen me hath seen the Father . . . Believest thou not that I am in the Father, and the Father in me? The words that I speak unto you, I speak not of myself; but the Father that dwelleth in me, he doeth the works (Jn. 14:9–10).

As a Prophet, the coming Messiah would be like Moses:

I will raise them up a Prophet from among their brethren, like unto thee [Moses], *and will put my words in his mouth, and he shall speak unto them all that I shall command him. And it shall come to pass, that whosoever will not hearken unto my words which he shall speak in my name, I will require it of him* (Dt. 18:18–19).

Moses was a remarkable character; and he was chosen, above all other prophets, to set forth in type the prophetic ministry of the coming Messiah. In these outstanding points, Christ was a prophet "like unto Moses." Moses was a *lawgiver, leader, king* (captain), *deliver, prophet* (God's spokesman) and *intercessor* for the people—he was the one with whom God spoke face to face. Never again did there arise a prophet like Moses (cp. Dt. 34:10–12; Num. 12:6–8). He was the only man in Jewish history who exercised the functions of prophet, priest and king in one ministry.

How right the people were who, when they had witnessed the miracle of Jesus feeding 5,000 people from a few loaves and fishes, said, "This is of a truth that prophet that should come into the world" (Jn. 6:14). "That prophet" is also referred to in John 1:21.

Although Moses was great, Christ was infinitely greater. Moses as a "servant" was "faithful"; Christ as the "son" was the perfect and omniscient Prophet (cp. Heb. 3:5–6) "Who was faithful to him that appointed him" (Heb. 3:2).

Peter summed up his sermon in the Temple with these words:

For Moses truly said unto the fathers, A prophet shall the Lord, your God, raise up unto you of your brethren, like unto me; him shall ye hear in all things, whatever he shall say unto you. And it shall come to pass that every soul, who will not hear that prophet, shall be destroyed from among the people (Acts 3:22–23).

Other references are made in both Testaments to the prophetic ministry of Christ. Isaiah 61:1 and Luke 4:18 refer to Christ's prophetic ministry, and both passages use the same words:

The Spirit of the Lord is upon me, because he hath anointed me to preach the gospel to the poor; he hath sent me to heal the brokenhearted, to preach deliverance to the captives, and recovering of sight to the blind, to set at liberty them that are bruised (Lk. 4:18; cp. Isa. 61:1).

Christ as Priest

The Old Testament priest, chosen by God, represented the people to God and offered sacrifices for their sins. He also had a ministry of compassion for the ignorant and erring (see Heb. 5:1–4). This priesthood, of which Aaron was the first high priest, was imperfect, for the priests were sinners themselves and had to first offer sacrifice for their own sins before they could offer sacrifice for the sins of the people (Heb. 5:3; 7:27; 9:7). Moreover, their priesthood was short-lived because the priesthood of each high priest was ended by his death (Heb. 7:23). Furthermore, their offerings were merely types, "For it is not possible that the blood of bulls and of goats should take away sins" (Heb. 10:4).

But in Christ, God's appointed High Priest, we have not only the perfect High Priest who lives forever, but One who gave Himself for our sins, the perfect offering, the once-for-all, complete atonement for the sins of humanity:

> *For such an high priest was fitting for us, who is holy, harmless, unde-*
> *filed, separate from sinners, and made higher than the heavens; Who*
> *needeth not daily, as those high priests, to offer up sacrifice, first for his*
> *own sins and then for the people's; for this he did once, when he offered*
> *up himself. For the law maketh men high priests who have infirmity, but*
> *the word of the oath, which was since the law, maketh the Son, who is*
> *consecrated for evermore* (Heb. 7:26–28).

By that one perfect offering on the cross, Christ "perfected forever" them that are saved through faith in Him (see Heb. 7:23–28; 9:25–28; 10:10–14). Most of the Book of Hebrews is devoted to the fact that in Christ Jesus, God has given us His perfect High Priest who offered the perfect offering to atone for the sins of the race, thereby giving eternal life to all who accept Him as their substitute and Savior. The Messiah gave His body and soul as an offering for sin and sinners (Isa. 53:5, 10).

In a sense, the Messiah was anointed to be *as a leper* when He bore the sins of the world. He was truly "made sin" for us (2 Cor. 5:21). Isaiah 53:4 intimates this, "we did esteem him stricken, smitten of God, and afflicted." Jerome translates the first phrase, "we thought him a leper." The word "stricken" was often used of the plague of leprosy. David Baron says of Isaiah 53:4, 'Stricken, smitten of God, afflicted'— every one of these three expressions was used of the plague of leprosy; and the phrases are intended to describe one suffering a terrible pun-ishment for sin." In the Messiah's case, it was for our sins, not His own, that He suffered so. Marvelous grace, that Christ actually was willing to become as a leper for us!

In this connection, it is interesting to note that the leper who was to be "cleansed" in the Old Testament economy was *anointed* (Lev. 14:15–20). One might conclude, therefore, that Christ, the Anointed of God, was not only anointed to be God's Prophet, Priest and King, but He also had an *anointing* to be the sin offering, and He literally became *sin (the leprous One)* for us.

Although the Aaronic priesthood continuously presented to the peo-ple their need of atonement for sins and that remission of sins could only be obtained through the shedding of blood (see Heb. 9:22), the one person chosen to picture the Messiah's eternal priesthood was not Aaron but Melchizedek (see Ps. 110:4; Heb. 5—7). Melchizedek, as a type of Christ, represented His eternal, unchanging priesthood; he "abideth a priest continually" (Heb. 7:3).

Christ as King

Yet have I set my king upon my holy hill of Zion (Ps. 2:6).

Since man is both an individual and a social unit, he needs a king (government) to supervise his community life. God, who first ruled the people of Israel through the patriarchs, later through "captains" (leaders like Moses and Joshua) and later still through "judges," finally consented to give them kings. In God's Messiah, we have the perfect King—the "KING OF KINGS, AND LORD OF LORDS" (Rev. 19:16)—who will have a wholly righteous, beneficent reign:

> *Behold, the days come, saith the LORD, that I will raise unto David a righteous Branch, and a King shall reign and prosper, and shall execute justice and righteousness in the earth . . . and this is his name whereby he shall be called, THE LORD OUR RIGHTEOUSNESS* (Jer. 23:5–6).
>
> *And the Spirit of the LORD shall rest upon him* [the Messiah] *and . . . with righteousness shall he judge* (Isa. 11:2, 4; cp. Num. 24:17; Zech. 9:9; etc.).

God selected three great men to picture the work of the Messiah as Prophet, Priest and King: Moses as prophet, Melchizedek as priest and David as king.

The term "Messiah" is found eighteen times in the Books of 1 and 2 Samuel, which narrate the life of David. Hannah, the mother of Samuel, had the honor of being the first one to use the word "Messiah" referring to the coming One, and to Christ as God's anointed King: "the LORD shall . . . give strength unto his king, and exalt the horn of his anointed" (1 Sam. 2:10).

The coming of the Messiah as King usually refers to His second advent, when He will establish His Kingdom reign of righteousness (see Isa. 11:1–10; Mic. 4:1–5; etc.).

Many psalms speak of the Messiah as the coming King (see Ps. 2; 45; 47; 72; etc.). In Psalm 2 we see the coronation of the Messiah as King on Mount Zion (v. 6) and His inheritance of the heathen nations (v. 8).

In Psalm 45 we see the majesty and beauty of the King and His glorious bride.

In Psalm 47 we see the Messiah as God and His coronation as King of the earth (vv. 2, 7).

Psalm 72 gives us the most complete picture in the psalms of the Messiah's coming Kingdom and His reign of righteousness:

1. The Messiah is identified as the King's Son (v. 1).
2. Messiah the King's perfect righteousness (vv. 2–4).
3. Messiah the King's wholesome reign (vv. 5–7).

4. Messiah the King's universal dominion (vv. 8–11).

5. Messiah the King's divine compassion (vv. 12–14).

6. Messiah the King's reign produces material and spiritual prosperity (vv. 15–17).

7. Messiah the King's reign produces perfect praise of the Lord God (vv. 18–19).

The Messiah is also presented as the Priest-King, "a priest upon his throne" (Zech. 6:13). This message to Joshua certainly looks beyond Joshua to the Messiah, for there are statements in the passage (Zech. 6:10–13) which can find their fulfillment only in one greater than man.

"Thus speaketh the LORD of hosts, saying, Behold, the man whose name is THE BRANCH" (v. 12) definitely identifies the message as being messianic. "He shall grow up out of his place" (v. 12) confirms that He will have a natural yet supernatural growth as a child (cp. Isa. 53:2). "And he shall build the temple of the LORD" (v. 12); Christ is doing this even now. "And he shall bear the glory" (v. 13), "the glory as of the only begotten of the Father" (Jn. 1:14). "And shall sit and rule upon his throne" (v. 13), as King and Priest, even as Melchizedek (Ps. 110:2, 4). "And the counsel of peace shall be between them both" (v. 13); as King, the Messiah will bring peace (Ps. 46:9; 72:7) and as Priest, He will bring peace through the blood of His cross (Col. 1:20).

Jeremiah 30:21 is another remarkable messianic passage giving a similar testimony. The Messiah will be the King-Priest; He will rule the people and "draw near and . . . approach unto God" as the perfect Mediator (cp. 1 Tim. 2:5).

Turning to the New Testament, the "Lion of the tribe of Judah, the Root of David" (Rev. 5:5) —Christ the King—is also presented as the One who "hath an unchangeable priesthood" (Heb. 7:24–28).

The New Testament Witness that Jesus is the Christ, the Anointed of God

In the New Testament, Jesus the Christ is clearly set forth as God's anointed Prophet (Jn. 17:8) who gives His people God's words; God's anointed Priest, "who through the eternal Spirit offered himself without spot to God [to] purge your conscience" (Heb; 9:14); and God's coming "KING OF KINGS, AND LORD OF LORDS" (Rev. 19:16).

In Hebrews 1:9, Christ is seen as the anointed of God: "Thou hast loved righteousness, and hated iniquity; therefore, God, even thy God, hath anointed thee with the oil of gladness above thy fellows."

In Luke 4:18, Christ stated that He was the One "anointed . . . to preach the gospel to the poor," the One of whom Isaiah spoke (Isa. 61:1). In several New Testament passages, Jesus is presented as Prophet, Priest and King:

And from Jesus Christ, who is the faithful witness [Prophet], *and the first begotten of the dead, and the prince of the kings of the earth* [King]. *Unto him that loveth us, and washed us from our sins in his own blood* [Priest] (Rev. 1:5).

God . . . Hath in these last days spoken unto us by his Son [Prophet] . . . *Who . . . when he had by himself purged our sins* [Priest], *sat down* [as King] *on the right hand of the Majesty on high* (Heb. 1:1–3).

Behold God's Branch

Other Bible teachers have called attention to the remarkable fourfold use of the messianic name "the Branch" in the Old Testament, and the frequent use of the word "behold" in connection with God's Messiah, the Branch. "Behold" is used as God's *Ecce Homo* in the Old Testament. Taken together, the phrase *Behold the Branch* presents a beautiful summary of the Christ of the four Gospels. Here is the fourfold use of the phrase as used of the Messiah in the Old Testament.

1. As the King

   Behold, the days come, saith the LORD, *that I will raise unto David a righteous Branch, and a King shall reign and prosper* (Jer. 23:5).

   Behold, thy King cometh unto thee (Zech. 9:9).

   This corresponds to the Gospel of Matthew, where Christ is presented as King.

2. As the Servant of the Lord

   Behold, I will bring forth my servant, the BRANCH (Zech. 3:8).

   This corresponds to the Gospel of Mark, where Christ is presented as the servant of the Lord.

3. As the Son of Man

   Thus speaketh the LORD *of hosts: saying, Behold, the man whose name is* THE BRANCH (Zech. 6:12).

   This corresponds to the Gospel of Luke, where Christ is presented as the ideal and the representative man.

4. As the Son of God

   Behold your God! (Isa. 40:9).

   In that day shall the branch of the LORD *be beautiful and glorious* (Isa. 4:2).

This corresponds to the Gospel of John, where Christ is presented
as the Son of God—God himself in the flesh.

These four uses of "the Branch" are the only four instances in the
Hebrew Scriptures (with the exception of Jer. 33:15, which is a repetition of
the thought in Jer. 23:5–6) where the Messiah is designated by the title, "the
Branch." Several times the Messiah is introduced in the Old Testament
with the word "Behold," as though to call special attention to Him.

Professor Godet writes:

Just as a gifted painter, who wished to immortalize for a family
the complete likeness of the illustrious father, would avoid any
attempt in combining in a single portrait the insignia of all the
various offices he had filled by representing him in the same picture as general and magistrate, as a man of science and as a father
of a family; but would prefer to paint four distinct portraits. So
the Holy Spirit, to preserve for mankind the perfect likeness of
Him who was its chosen representative, God in man, used means
to impress upon the minds of the writers of the Gospels, four different images.

All of these four accounts of the life of Christ present Him as the
Messiah—God's perfect Prophet, Priest, King and the Son of God—yet
each has a different emphasis. In Matthew, He is *King*; in Mark, He is
the servant of Jehovah; in Luke, He is the *Son of man*; and in John, He is
the *Son of God*.

Other Names of the Messiah in the Old Testament

There are scores of names of the Messiah in the Old Testament.
Following are a few.

In Isaiah, the Messiah is frequently called *the servant of the Lord* or
"my servant" (see Isa. 42:1; 52:13; etc.). As the servant of the Lord
(Jehovah), He is the exponent of righteousness and true humility, the
teacher and Redeemer of mankind. He fulfills all of God's desires;
hence, He is:

The second Adam—the perfect Man
The second Israel—the perfect Servant
The second Moses—the perfect Prophet
The second David—the perfect King
The second High Priest—the perfect High Priest

The growing purposes of God toward the whole human race, which
were manifested in the creation of Adam, the election of Israel, the raising

up of Moses, the appointment of Aaron and the call of David are "brought to their full completion by, in and through Christ" (Delitzsch).

Ezekiel presented the Messiah as *the Shepherd of Israel* (see Ezek. 34:23; 37:24). In Ezekiel, "David" is used as a name of the Messiah. "David" means *beloved*.

Christ, the truly beloved of the Father, took both the name and character of the true Shepherd (see Jn. 10).

The Messiah is frequently called the "angel of the LORD," God's messenger (see Jud. 2:1; 6:12–13). He is also called the "stone" or the "rock" (Isa. 8:14); the "corner" (Isa. 28:16); the "nail" (Isa. 22:21–25); the "battle bow" (Zech. 10:4); "Shiloh" (Gen. 49:10); the "star" (Num. 24:17); etc.

The Name "Jesus" in the Old Testament

In an enlightening study, *Yeshua In The Tenach* (*The Name Jesus in the Old Testament*), Arthur E. Glass points out the amazing fact that the name "Jesus" is actually hidden in the Old Testament; yet it "is found about one hundred times from Genesis to Habakkuk . . . Every time the Old Testament uses the word *salvation* (especially with the Hebrew suffix meaning 'my,' 'thy' or 'his'), with very few exceptions (when the word is used in an impersonal sense) it is identically the same word as Yeshua (Jesus) used in Matthew 1:21." According to Glass, "This is actually what the angel said to Joseph: 'And she shall bring forth a son, and thou shalt call his name Yeshua (salvation), for he shall save his people from their sins.'"

In Psalm 9:14, David said, "I will rejoice in thy salvation." What he actually said was, "I will rejoice in thy Yeshua [Jesus]." In Isaiah 12:2–3, salvation is mentioned three times, presenting three great facets of Jesus and His salvation. They are presented here (quoting Glass) as they read in the Hebrew, with Jesus as the embodiment and the personification of the word salvation:

Behold, the mighty one [or God the mighty One] is my Yeshua [a reference to Jesus in His preincarnation, eternal existence, cp. Jn. 1:1]; I will trust and not be afraid; for Jah-Jehovah is my strength and my song: He also is become my Yeshua [Jesus, the Word made flesh, Jn. 1:14]. Therefore, with joy shall ye draw water out of the wells of Yeshua [Jesus crucified, waters of salvation flowing from Calvary, cp. Jn. 7:37–39].

Prophecies Proving
That the Messiah Is God

The Dual Nature of the Messiah

For a correct comprehension of the person of the Messiah, it is necessary to understand that He has a *dual nature* but is a single personality. He is very God and perfect man; He is the God-Man, God and man in one indivisible personality. His humanity is seen in such names and titles as Son of man, Son of David, Son of Abraham, etc. His deity is seen in such names and titles as Son of God, God, Lord, Jehovah, El, Elohim, etc. The Bible reveals the Messiah (Christ) to be God manifest in the flesh.

The Deity of Christ as Presented in Hebrews Chapter 1

In the first six verses of Hebrews chapter 1, ten characteristics are presented about Christ, all of which prove and establish the fact of His deity.

1. Christ (the Messiah) is called God's Son, in contrast to the prophets who were only men, even though they were inspired men: "God, who . . . spoke in time past unto the fathers by the prophets, Hath in these last days spoken unto us by his Son" (vv. 1–2).

2. Christ is "heir of all things" (v. 2). He is the Son; therefore, He is the heir.

3. The "worlds" (universe) were made through Him (Christ) [v. 2]. This not only proves His preexistence but reveals Him as the active agent in creation. A parallel passage is John 1:1–3: "all things were made by him [Christ]; and without him was not anything made that was made" (v. 3).

4. He is identified with the glory of God as much as the brightness of the sun is identified with the sun: "Who, being the brightness of his glory, and the express image of his person" (v. 3).

5. He is identified with the character of God as much as the impression of a seal exactly reproduces the seal: "the express image of his person" (v. 3).

6. He is the One who upholds the vast, infinite universe, which is the work of an omnipotent God: "upholding all things by the word of his power (v. 3; cp. Col. 1:16–17, "For by him were all things created . . . and by him all things consist [Gr., *are held together*]."

7. Christ accomplished the redemption of all humanity alone. No sinful man, not even a perfect man, could redeem a race of billions of lost sinners. It takes an infinite sacrifice to atone for a world of sinners: "when he had by himself purged [made purification of] our sins" (v. 3).

8. He now occupies the highest position in the universe next to the Father, at God's right hand, sharing with God the Father the eternal throne: "he . . . sat down on the right hand of the Majesty on high" (v. 3). That Christ, the Lamb of God, shares the eternal throne is evident from Revelation 22:1: "the throne [singular] of God and of the Lamb."

9. He is much better than the angels: "Being made so much better than the angels" (v. 4).

10. Again, the Father-Son relationship of the Father and the Messiah is established. Even the angels are commanded to worship the Messiah: "let all the angels of God worship him" (v. 6). The Scriptures command that only God is to be worshiped (Mt. 4:10). "Thou art my Son . . . I will be to him a Father, and he shall be to me a Son" (v. 5) is the Father's testimony to the Son.

In the remainder of the first chapter of Hebrews (together with the Old Testament Scriptures from which quotations are made in this first chapter of Hebrews), the Messiah is called by three primary names and titles of God used in the Old Testament and by the two primary names of deity used in the New Testament.

In verse 8, God the Father, speaking to God the Son (the Messiah), calls Him God (Gr., *Theos*). Verse 8 is a quotation from Psalm 45:6, where the primary name of God, *Elohim*, is used of the Messiah: "Thy throne, O God [Heb., *Elohim*], is forever and ever."

In Hebrews 1:10, God the Father, still speaking to and about the Son (the Messiah), calls Him Lord (Gr., *Kurios*). This is a quotation from Psalm 102:25–27 which refers to *Jehovah* (see Ps. 102:16, 19, 21–22). Consider this passage:

And Thou, Lord, in the beginning hast laid the foundation of the earth; and the heavens are the works of thine hands. They shall perish, but thou remainest; and they all shall become old as doth a garment, And as a vesture shalt thou fold them up, and they shall be changed; but thou art the same, and thy years shall not fail (Heb. 1:10–12).

Notice that in these verses the Father (as in verse 8) is still speaking to the Son; the Father says that the Son is the Creator of the universe ("the heavens are the works of thine hands," v. 10); and the Father says that the Son is eternal, unchangeable. The universe will get old as does a used garment, but of the Son (the Messiah) the Father says, "thy years shall not fail" (v. 12).

The writer of the Book of Hebrews added two additional inspired comments concerning the Messiah: "But to which of the angels said he [God the Father] at any time, Sit on my right hand" (v. 13), again showing the exalted position of the Messiah at God's right hand; and "until I make thine enemies thy footstool" (v. 13), assuring all of the Messiah's eternal victory.

Since God the Father has testified so emphatically in this chapter of the deity of Christ and has given us 15 statements that fully set forth His deity, our eternal salvation depends on our accepting this truth: "If ye believe not that I am he [the Lord Jehovah], ye shall die in your sins" (Jn. 8:24). In this passage, Christ used the words "I am," which is the meaning of the name Jehovah (see Ex. 3:14–15), thus identifying Himself as the Jehovah of the Old Testament.

Old Testament Statements Concerning the Deity of the Messiah

Turning to the Old Testament predictions and comparing them with their New Testament fulfillments, we discover that Jehovah calls the Messiah His "fellow" (equal): "Awake, O sword, against my shepherd, and against the man who is my fellow, saith the LORD of hosts" (Zech. 13:7).

In the New Testament, Christ said the same thing when He stated, "I and my Father are one" (Jn. 10:30). Paul, inspired by the Holy Spirit, testified that Christ is equal with God: "Christ Jesus . . . being in the form of God, thought it not robbery [a thing to be grasped] to be equal with God" (Phil. 2:6).

Isaiah 9:6 forecasts the Messiah's humanity, deity and kingship. Names of deity are bestowed on the coming Messiah which none can mistake:

For unto us a child is born [the Messiah's humanity], *unto us a son is given* [His eternal Sonship in the Triunity] . . . *and his name shall be called Wonderful, Counselor, The Mighty God* [Heb., *El Gibor*], *The Everlasting Father* [both names of God], *The Prince of Peace.*

A name in Hebrew expresses that which a person is; being called something means being that thing. Therefore, when the Messiah is called by the name "The Mighty God," it means that He is the Mighty God.

The Messiah is called God (Heb., *El, Elohim*) in the Old Testament: "Say unto the cities of Judah, Behold your God [Elohim]! Behold, the Lord GOD [Elohim] will come with strong hand" (Isa. 40:9–10).

In Psalm 47:7–8, we read of the Messiah's second advent: "For God [Elohim] is the King of all the earth . . . God [Elohim] reigneth over the nations" (cp. 1 Cor. 15:24–25; Rev. 11:15; 19:16).

The Messiah is also called Jehovah in the Old Testament. In Zechariah 2:10, we read that the Lord (Jehovah) said, "lo, I come, and I will dwell in the midst of thee." Psalm 47:2 says, "For the LORD [Jehovah] Most High is . . . a great King over all the earth." The context shows that this is a messianic psalm, looking forward to the second advent of Christ.

In Jeremiah 23:6, we read that the Messiah "shall be called, THE LORD [JEHOVAH] OUR RIGHTEOUSNESS." Psalm 102:16 tells us that "The LORD [Jehovah] . . . shall appear in his glory." In Zechariah 14:9, we read that "the LORD [Jehovah] shall be King over all the earth."

To prove that it is Jehovah in the flesh who is the King, Zechariah 14:3–4 tells us, "Then shall the LORD [Jehovah] go forth . . . and his feet shall stand in that day upon the Mount of Olives."

There can be no mistaking the meaning of Zechariah 12:10: "They shall look upon me [Jehovah] whom they have pierced." This is a direct reference to the crucified Messiah.

Isaiah 40:3 is a clear prediction that the Messiah is called both Jehovah (LORD) and Elohim (God): "The voice of him that crieth in the wilderness, Prepare ye the way of the LORD [Jehovah], make straight in the desert a highway for our God [Elohim]." This Scripture is quoted in the New Testament, showing its fulfillment in Christ and in John the Baptist, His forerunner (see Mt. 3:1–3).

In Zephaniah 3:15, we learn that it is Jehovah himself, the "Holy One" of Israel, who will be in their midst: "the King of Israel, even the LORD [Jehovah], is in the midst of thee."

In the New Testament, Jesus claimed to be the great "I AM" of the Old Testament. Jehovah said of Himself in Isaiah 43:10: "Ye are my witnesses, saith the LORD [Jehovah], and my servant whom I have chosen, that ye may know and believe me, and understand that I am he."

It is, therefore, very significant that Christ made the same claim: "that . . . ye may believe that I am he" (Jn. 13:19; cp. Mk. 13:6; Jn. 4:26; 8:24; 13:19; etc.). Jesus frequently used the expression "I am" in connection with some special revelation of His person or work:

"I am the light of the world" (Jn. 8:12).

"I am the door" (Jn. 10:9).

"I am the good shepherd" (Jn. 10:14).

"I am the way, the truth, and the life" (Jn. 14:6).

Adonai, another name for God, is also assigned to the Messiah in the Old Testament: "Behold, I will send my messenger, and he shall prepare the way before me; and the Lord [Heb., *Adonai*], whom ye seek, shall suddenly come to his temple" (Mal. 3:1).

The "messenger" who prepared the way for the coming of the Lord (*Adonai*) was John the Baptist; and the Lord for whom he prepared the way was the Messiah, Jesus: "The LORD [Jehovah] said unto my Lord [Adonai], Sit thou at my right hand until I make thine enemies thy footstool" (Ps. 110:1).

On the day of Pentecost, Peter quoted this passage in his sermon to prove both the Messiahship and the deity of Christ (Acts 2:34–36. In Matthew 22:41–45, Jesus himself proved to the Pharisees that the Messiah is not only the son of David, He is also his Lord (*Adonai*).

The Old Testament teaches the preexistence of the Messiah: "his name shall be continued as long as the sun" (Ps. 72:17). The original Hebrew of this text reads: "Before the sun was, his name [was] Yinon." This is the only occurrence in Scripture of the word "Yinon," and all ancient Jewish commentators agree that it is a name of the Messiah.

In Proverbs 8:22–24, we read of the preexistence of the Messiah: "The LORD possessed me in the beginning of his way, before his works of old.

I was set up from everlasting, from the beginning, or ever the earth was." That this is a description of the eternal Messiah is beyond doubt.

In perfect agreement with the Old Testament, the New Testament also teaches the preexistence of Christ, the eternal Word: "In the beginning was the Word, and the Word was with God, and the Word was God. The same was in the beginning with God" (Jn. 1:1–2).

The Old Testament presents the Messiah as "the glory of the LORD," a phrase signifying deity: "And the glory of the LORD shall be revealed, and all flesh shall see it" (Isa. 40:5; cp. vv. 3–4 which prove v. 5 to be messianic).

In the New Testament, we read of the Messiah's incarnation: "And the Word was made flesh, and dwelt among us (and we beheld his glory, the glory as of the only begotten of the Father), full of grace and truth" (Jn. 1:14).

New Testament Statements Concerning the Deity of Christ

We have seen from Hebrews chapter 1 that the New Testament teaches the deity of Christ (the Messiah). This teaching of Christ's deity pervades the entire New Testament and can be seen in scores of direct statements and hundreds of references. Some of the inferences of Christ's deity are as follows:

1. His power to forgive sin proves His deity (Mk. 2:10).
2. His right to receive worship proves His deity (Mt. 2:11; 8:2; 9:18; 14:33; etc.).
3. His supernatural powers prove His deity (see all His miracles as recorded in the Gospels, e.g., Mk. 2:11; 3:5, 10–11; etc.).
4. His sinless character proves His deity (Heb. 7:26; 1 Pet. 2:22; 1 Jn. 3:5). In Luke 18:19, the Lord taught, indirectly, that none should call Him good unless they admit He is God, for there is none good except God.
5. His atoning death proves His deity, for none but God could atone for the race (Heb. 2:9).
6. His bodily resurrection proves His deity (Rom. 1:4).
7. He gave many promises which require deity for their fulfillment (see Mt. 11:28–29; 28:19–20; Jn. 14:23).
8. Men are to trust Him even as they do the Father, thereby affirming His deity (Jn. 14:1–3).
9. He is the Creator and Sustainer of the universe, positions which could only be attributed to deity (Jn. 1:1–3; Col. 1:16–17).

10. He has all the characteristics of deity: omnipresence, omni-
science, omnipotence, etc. (see Mt. 28:18, 20; Jn. 3:13; 14:23;
16:30; etc.).

Note the striking testimony of Christ's deity in Luke 1:68 and 76. See
also John 20:28; Romans 9:5; 1 Corinthians 2:8; Colossians 1:14, 17; 1
Timothy 6:14–16; Titus 2:13; Hebrews 1; etc.

The Triunity

That the Messiah should be God and yet be sent by God is a mystery
unravelled only in the teaching of the Triunity. God is one God existing
in three persons: Father, Son (the Messiah) and Holy Spirit.

Following are some references which directly teach or intimate the
doctrine of the Triunity.

In Genesis 1:1, the word "God" (*Elohim*) is in the plural and is fol-
lowed by the verb "created," which is in the singular, thus intimating a
plurality of persons in the Godhead who are one.

In Deuteronomy 6:4, the word for "one" (God) is *echad*, which is the
word for a compound unity, not an absolute unity. "Echad" is used in
Genesis 2:24, which teaches that Adam and Eve (a man and his wife)
shall be "one [*echad*] flesh"—two persons as one (see also Gen. 11:5–6;
Num. 13:23; Jud. 20:1–2).

There are many direct statements concerning the Triunity in the Old
Testament, such as Isaiah 11:2; 42:1; 48:16–17; 61:1; 63:7–10; Zechariah
2:10; etc. In Numbers 6:24–27, note that the singular "my name" in
verse 27 follows the threefold use of the name LORD in verses 24–26.

Many Scriptures intimate the Triunity, such as Genesis 1:26–27,
where God says, "Let us," implying more than one person in the
Godhead (see also Gen. 3:22; 11:5–7; Isa. 6:8).

The Triunity is clearly taught in the New Testament in such instances
as Matthew 3:16–17; 28:19–20; John 14:16; 2 Corinthians 13:14;
Ephesians 4:4–6; Hebrews 9:14; and Revelation 1:4–5.

Chapter Eight

Prophecies From the Old Testament Fulfilled in Christ

The Bible is unique in its *type-pictures* of the coming Messiah as well as in its distinct and definite prophecies.

The Bible is unique in at least seven ways. First, it alone, of all the books in the world, has genuine prophecy. Second, the Bible alone contains an intricate system of "types" in the Old Testament which are fulfilled in the New Testament. Third, the Bible alone contains the record of genuine, credible miracles, fully attested to by adequate witnesses. Fourth, of all the books in the world, the Bible alone presents the perfect character, the Messiah. Fifth, the Bible alone, of all national history books, portrays its characters without bias and presents them as they are, with their weaknesses and failures as well as their strong points. Sixth, the Bible alone, of all ancient books, is in agreement with all the facts of nature and true scientific discoveries to which it refers, even though it was written thousands of years before the modern scientific era. Seventh, although written by nearly 40 human authors, the Bible has a phenomenal unity which shows the superintendence of its divine Author.

A *type* is a divinely created illustration of spiritual truth. A person, place, thing, event or a series of events becomes, by divine foresight and planning, an object lesson—a *picture* with corresponding details— of its anti-type (fulfillment). God and Christ, Satan and Antichrist, believers and unbelievers, the yielded Christian life and the world are just a few subjects of biblical types. "Even where no direct prediction is found," comments A. T. Pierson, "indirect forecasts (through types) referring to Christ may be distinctly traced all through the Bible." How true! Types of Christ—prophetic pictures giving indirect forecasts— abound in the Old Testament.

The cross of Christ has perhaps more types previewing and prefiguring the sacrifice of the Son of God than anything else in the Bible. Every Passover lamb slain (with its attendant ceremonies of the sprinkling of the blood of the lamb on the door posts, the eating of the roasted lamb, etc., (see Ex. 12:1–13), every Levitical offering brought to the altar and sacrificed (see Lev. 1–6) and every other blood offering presented "from the hour of Abel's altar-fire down to the last Passover of the passion week, pointed as with flaming finger to Calvary's Cross! . . . And there we see the convergence of a thousand lines of prophecy (indirect forecasts) . . . as in one burning focal point of dazzling glory" (A. T. Pierson).

When the Passover lamb was roasted, "a spit was thrust lengthwise through its body, and another transversely from shoulder to shoulder; every Passover lamb was thus transfixed *on a cross*. In like manner, when Moses lifted up the brazen serpent (Num. 21) it was not on a pole but on a *banner staff*—i.e., *a cross*" (A. T. Pierson, *Many Infallible Proofs*, p. 204).

Pictures of Christ abound in the Old Testament

In Genesis (especially rich in prophetic forecasts of Christ), *Adam* is presented as the head of God's creation, a type of Christ as Head of the new creation (see 1 Cor. 15:45–49). The *ark* was the only means of saving people from the judgment of the flood (Gen. 6—9). Christ is the ark of salvation; all who come to Him by faith are saved from the coming flood of God's judgment against sin. The *offering of Isaac* (Gen. 22) is an especially rich type of the offering up of Jesus by His Father. The *life of Joseph*—beloved of his father but hated and rejected by his brothers (Gen. 37)—is an amazing picture, with over 100 corresponding features, of the Lord Jesus Christ, who, likewise, was beloved of His Father but hated and rejected by His brethren. Joseph was sent to the Gentiles from whom he obtained a bride and was the means of feeding multitudes and saving them from destruction (Gen. 39—47). Christ, rejected by His brethren (the Jews), has been preached to the Gentiles, and vast multi-tudes have been preserved and fed the bread of life by Him. Joseph finally revealed himself to his brethren and became the means of pre-serving them. So too Christ, in the latter days, will reveal Himself to Israel and save many of them (see Zech. 12:10; Rom. 11:25–26).

In Exodus, the *Passover lamb* and the *life and ministry of Moses* are out-standing types of Christ. Moses, a shepherd in his youth and at first rejected by his brethren, fled to a Gentile country where he married a Gentile bride. Later, when he returned to liberate Israel, he was accepted as their leader and led them out of bondage in Egypt with great victory. This type of Christ is thrilling, for it speaks of Christ's rejection at His first coming to Israel and His eventual acceptance by and leadership over Israel at His second coming (see Acts 7:22–37, especially v. 35).

The *life of David* in 1 and 2 Samuel is a similar picture of the Messiah. David was a shepherd in his youth; was rejected by Saul, who sought to kill him; and was later accepted by the nation, anointed and crowned as their king. He is a type of the greater David who at first was the "good shepherd" who gave His life for His sheep and who later will reign as King.

Aaron and *Melchizedek* picture Christ as High Priest. *Moses* and *Samuel* (and the other prophets) foreshadow Christ as the great Prophet.

Christ explained that the *brazen serpent*, uplifted before the people as a means of deliverance from the judgment of death because of their sin (see Num. 21:5–9), was a type of His work of salvation through His cross (see Jn. 3:14–18).

Jonah, swallowed by the whale, experiencing a type of death and resur-rection, and then preaching to the Gentiles, is a picture of the Messiah who was "three days and three nights" in the heart of the earth and who came forth—as Jonah did—in resurrection. In Matthew 12:40, Christ used Jonah's experience to illustrate a type of His own death and resurrection.

The *Tabernacle* (Ex. 25—31; 35—40) is one of the most extensive and meaningful of all the types. Its priesthood, offerings, furniture and arrangement are all symbolic of Christ and the believer's approach to God through Christ.

1. The brazen altar stands for atonement by blood.
2. The laver of cleansing stands for sanctification through the "wash-ing of water by the word" (Eph. 5:26).
3. The table of show bread is a type of Christ as the food and strength of His people.

4. The golden lampstand with its seven branches is a type of Christ, the light of the world.

5. The altar of incense represents prayers and supplications ascending to the throne of God (cp. Rev. 8:3).

6. The mercy seat in the holy of holies represents Christ as the only means of justification and access to the presence of God (see Lk. 18:13, where the publican's prayer, "God be merciful to me a sinner," can be paraphrased, "God, meet me at the mercy seat").

7. The ark of the covenant in the holy of holies speaks of Christ as our Representative and Mediator at the right hand of God. The ark was made of wood and covered with pure gold (Ex. 25:10–11). This speaks of the humanity (wood) and deity (pure gold) of Christ. The ark contained three things: "the golden pot that had manna, and Aaron's rod that budded, and the tables of the covenant" (Heb. 9:4). These speak in types and pictures of the Messiah as the bread that came down from Heaven, of His resurrection and of His perfect keeping of the Law. In His heart alone the Law remains unbroken.

8. The Tabernacle itself speaks of the incarnation, Christ dwelling among His people (see Jn. 1:14). The boards, sockets, curtains, coverings—everything connection with the Tabernacle and its service—are, in some way, types of Christ.

The *feasts of the Lord* set forth in Leviticus 23 are a beautiful and progressive revelation of the work of Christ for His people and the unfolding of the plan of God, through Christ, especially as it relates to Israel.

And so, the wondrous story of the types in the Old Testament unfolds, giving us vast and understandable revelations of the coming Messiah and of His person and work.

Messianic typology in the Old Testament opens a door to the fuller comprehension of the Messiah, the Christ of God. The Book of Hebrews shows clearly that these amazing types in the Old Testament are not the result of mere chance but were divinely planned to give pictures of Christ and His offering on the cross (see Heb. 5—10). Moses, when he was about to construct the Tabernacle, was "admonished of God . . . to make . . . all things according to the pattern shown to thee" (Heb. 8:5). In other words, God planned the types—lives of men, institutions such as the Tabernacle and his worship, and events in the history of Israel—to serve as illustrations.

Conclusion

In conclusion, the following points are very clear. First, there is genuine prophecy in the Bible, and in the Bible alone. Second, this prophecy proves beyond all doubt that Jesus of Nazareth, the central character of the New Testament, is the predicted Messiah of the Old Testament. Third, the Messiah (Christ) is God manifested in the flesh. Fourth, the Bible is the Word of God. Fifth, the God of the Bible is the only true God. Sixth, the eternal salvation of man's soul is accomplished solely by trusting Christ and His redeeming work on the cross.

Since these great realizations of prophecy are true and provable, it is the duty of each individual to trust Christ for his own salvation, surrender to His Lordship and live for Him. Since the Bible tells us that man's eternal destiny depends on trusting Christ— "He that believeth on the Son hath everlasting life; and he that believeth not the Son shall not see life, but the wrath of God abideth on him" (Jn. 3:36)—it should be our greatest desire to witness to others of these facts and make them aware that "there is no other name under heaven given among men, whereby we must be saved" (Acts 4:12).

**THESE ARE WRITTEN, THAT YE MIGHT BELIEVE
THAT JESUS IS THE CHRIST, THE SON OF GOD;
AND THAT BELIEVING YE MIGHT HAVE LIFE
THROUGH HIS NAME** (Jn. 20:31).